C T STUDD
AND
PRISCILLA

By the same author:

God Can Do It Here
Something's Happening
I Will Heal Their Land

C T STUDD

AND

PRISCILLA

United to Fight for Jesus

Eileen Vincent

STL BOOKS
BROMLEY KENT

WEC PUBLICATIONS
GERRARDS CROSS

KINGSWAY PUBLICATIONS
EASTBOURNE

Biblical quotations are from the
Authorised Version, Crown copyright
or from the New International Version
© International Bible Society 1973, 1978, 1984.
Published by Hodder & Stoughton.

British Library Cataloguing in Publication Data

Vincent, Eileen.
C.T. Studd and Priscilla.
1. Christian missions. Studd, C.T. —
Biographies
I. Title
266' .0092'4
ISBN 0 86065 589 X (Kingsway)
0 900828 50 1 (WEC)
0 85078 053 6 (STL)

STL Books are published by Send the Light
(Operation Mobilisation), PO Box 48, Bromley, Kent

WEC Publications are produced by WEC International,
Bulstrode, Gerrards Cross, Bucks. SL9 8SZ

Production and printing in Great Britain for
KINGSWAY PUBLICATIONS LTD
Lottbridge Drove, Eastbourne, E. Sussex BN23 6NT
by Nuprint Ltd, Harpenden, Herts AL5 4SE.

CONTENTS

List of Illustrations

Acknowledgements

Foreword by Patrick Johnstone

Introduction

1.	A Success Story	15
2.	A Brand New Life	19
3.	Eton Days	24
4.	Caught Out	29
5.	Decision Time	37
6.	The Confident Generation	43
7.	The Flame is Lit	50
8.	The Chinese Training School	61
9.	What is this Waste?	75
10.	An Encounter of the Heart	80
11.	Finding his own Identity	90
12.	Identification and Suffering in China	97
13.	Ministry in the United States	109
14.	Indian Delight	117
15.	Fifty Not Out!	126

16. Priscilla Alone   134
17. A Continuing Sacrifice   138
18. Death to Himself   142
19. Determined Against All Odds   150
20. A New Priscilla   157
21. Paying the Price to Enter the Land   163
22. Dark Kilo Days   171
23. The Heart of Africa   180
24. Establishing a Bridgehead   191
25. One Handful of Blessing Mixed With
       Two of Trial   199
26. Priscilla the Mainstay   211
27. Incoming Friendly   223
28. Much Fruit   236

*Important Dates in the Lives of
   C T Studd and Priscilla*   240

Sources of Information   242

Notes   247

Index   249

LIST OF ILLUSTRATIONS

C T Studd the cricketer   31
Map of China   62
The Cambridge Seven   65
P S Smith with C T and Priscilla   72
Priscilla shortly after her conversion   82
Pauline, Edith, Dorothy and Grace   122
Map of Belgian Congo   181
C T Studd playing his banjo   184
C T Studd at work in the Congo   187
Every man brought his own deckchair   193
C T Studd in 1916   203
Priscilla in 1921   212
Priscilla at the Keswick Convention   219
C T Studd in 1929   239

ACKNOWLEDGEMENTS

My sincere thanks go to the WEC Publications Committee. First of all to John Mills, who initiated my interest in the book. Then to Chris Scott, who has provided a continuous stream of information and patiently checked the manuscript. I owe much to Chris for the book's accuracy. My husband Alan is my most faithful critic, and deserves all my thanks. Without his encouragement and constant inspiration this book would not have been written.

FOREWORD

Charles and Priscilla Studd: a man and a woman of God! With them nothing was done by half measures. They were controversial radicals in their day—yet what an example they set us who follow after them! They were true crusaders for Jesus who lived and breathed for one thing only: the glory of God in the evangelisation of the whole world. They wanted hell emptied and heaven filled. They gave up wealth, comfort, family togetherness and their very selves that this noble objective be realised.

The white-hot vision fired their voices and pens to stir lethargic tunnel-visioned churches and self-centred believers to action. Who can tell how many have marched out in full-time Christian service and into missions as a result of their challenges? As well as the mission they themselves founded—WEC International—I know of possibly ten mission agencies that have indirectly come into being as a result of their ministry. Many of these are the outgrowth of WEC's work in other countries. 'CT' and 'Mother Studd' vigorously promoted concepts such as unevangelised peoples and the evangelisation of the world in our generation— concepts widely espoused by missions today.

Yet they were human. They had their weaknesses. The author has handled this faithfully and with sensitivity. But it was their spiritual greatness which magnifies these, and they must not allow us to detract from their achievements. Weapons forged for battle with Satan were sometimes aimed at others. They were frequently the subject of controversy— especially in their later years. Every action of CT's inspired either intense zeal and loyalty, or fervent hostility. No one could be neutral with him! Yet what giants they were! Who are we to criticise if we are unwilling to exercise the same mighty faith, show the same selfless daring and make the same costly sacrifices? To use CT's words, are we 'passengers in the coaches of the Church' or 'pushers of the war machines of God'?

It is their heart for God and his Cause that shines through these pages. May ours glow with a similiar passion for an unevangelised world. There is much for us to learn from these warrior saints. May Charles Studd's rallying cry do just that to us:

> Let nobody mistake our objective, the devil will seek to drag many red herrings across the scent. Our objective is *The evangelisation of all the unevangelised regions of the world*. For that we have the divine warrant of God's Word, for anything short of that, however prettily or fancifully expressed, we have no authority nor attraction. *We want Jesus back again*.... We care not by whom this glorious end is accomplished. Whether our share is great or insignificant matters not. Only we shall take and give no rest to any till this thing is done.

Patrick Johnstone
Deputy International Secretary
WEC International

INTRODUCTION
THE END OF LITTLE GAMES

An American newspaper correspondent watched as a city was taken by insurgent communists. As the flames rose all around, he wrote:

> Tonight Shanghai is burning,
> And I am burning too.
> But there's no death so real
> As the death inside of you.
> Some men die by shrapnel
> And some go down in flames,
> But most men die inch by inch
> Playing little games. [1]

C T Studd never came into that category. He saw past the 'little games' to a more deadly war involving perpetual flames and eternally dying people. In his mind's eye he saw the lost burning in hell—he could not sit by and do nothing.

The story of C T Studd is thoroughly relevant for today. The flames of hell are licking through the cracks of our comfortable, civilised society. One city will not satiate hell's lust. The whole world is in danger.

This book is written to urge Christians today to respond to

the desperate cry of those without Christ. Your next-door neighbour, or some forgotten tribe no matter where they are, urgently need to know what you know.

The devil is not very concerned by individuals being born again. What really troubles him are those who actually do something, who wage war against his kingdom. Satan will concentrate all his offensive to keep Christians, who have the potential power to decimate his kingdom, from ever rising up to do anything, except to go to church on Sunday.

The average Christian life is lived in a dichotomy. One part 'normal' daily life, and a lesser part, 'spiritual'. The spiritual part is so often crowded into a few moments of the day and rarely invades the normal, which is set solid in secular attitudes and interests.

When C T Studd had an encounter with God his double life came to an abrupt end. From that day forward he totally belonged to Jesus. No sacrifice was too much. His normal daily life was no longer for himself but, with every faculty and ability, he served God. C T Studd said, *'If Jesus Christ be God and died for me, then no sacrifice can be too great for me to make for him.'*

May the story of Charles Studd and Priscilla stir your heart to the same zeal and sacrificial commitment, so that before Jesus comes again a mighty harvest will be reaped. The powers of darkness will be pushed back by dedicated soldiers of Christ who follow in their train.

These are crucial days. It is essential that the church rises up out of lethargy and, by the power of the Spirit, equips herself afresh with zeal to boldly proclaim the gospel. Zeal and Holy Spirit boldness caused the early church to explode in its generation. The ways of God have not changed. May he come upon us as he did upon them in a powerful baptism of fire, to set our hearts ablaze and loose our tongues. The church today has more resources and opportunity for learning than any previous generation. We cannot plead ignorance.

We do not need one more scrap of knowledge. God waits for obedience.

The lives of Charles and Priscilla are an indictment against the believing evangelical church, where men die inch by inch. Let us leave our little games—even our religious games—and get on with the task.

Eileen Vincent
November 1987

CHAPTER ONE

A SUCCESS STORY

SOMETHING INCREDIBLE must have gripped him. What on earth could cause a wealthy young man to bury himself in the depths of China—then, with his indomitable wife and four young daughters, to go to India? As if that was not enough, after more than thirty years of abandoned, tireless service for Jesus, when he was as good as finished in his fifty-third year, he left his wife at home and pioneered in the great forests of central Africa. To crown it all, in co-operation with the same fearless lady, he founded a worldwide mission which continues today to touch the ends of the earth.

Charles Thomas Studd was born into a wealthy family on December 2nd, 1860, during the reign of Queen Victoria. This man, whose name was to become famous and whose cricketing achievements were to make him a national hero, was nurtured in the predictable security of the landed gentry of his day.

It is hard for us in this ever-changing intercontinental age to appreciate the stability of an era where life continued the same as it always had. The rich were rich and the poor were poor. Covetousness seemed not to have been discovered. One's place in life was accepted almost without question and prepared for with diligence. Daughters went into service, and sons learned a trade, or they went to Eton then on to Oxbridge and became gentlemen.

Edward Studd, Charles' father, was a clever, enterprising man who had made enough money for a double fortune. He owned two indigo plantations in Bihar, North India. Indigo was big business — the only available blue dye in the world.

After the death of his young wife he met Dora Thomas who came from a well-placed family in Bedfordshire, and there he married her in 1856. A new life began, generously funded by his Indian wealth. Finally the family settled at Tedworth House in Wiltshire, a grand, spacious Georgian manor house with adequate parkland for a race course and a cricket pitch. Four sons had been born who, as soon as they were able, were strapped into the saddle to accompany their father in his greatest enjoyment. Horses were the passion of his life; he devoted himself to breeding, hunting, training and racing them. His new property provided him with ample scope for developing his sporting interests. With his eye set to win the Grand National, he built up a stud of twenty horses, and in 1886 his horse Salamander came in first — the pinnacle of racing success was his. The day ended crowned with extravagant celebrations.

What a happy man Edward Studd must have been! His family of four had now increased to seven — six sons and one daughter. Charles was the third son. Edward appeared to lack nothing; he enjoyed the enviable life of a rich country gentleman surrounded by his children, who were growing up knowing nothing but plenty, luxury and pleasure. Edward Studd was an enthusiastic character who enjoyed his social and sporting life to the full.

At the tender age of seven years, Charlie, with his two elder brothers, was sent off to preparatory school at Cheam. From Cheam they graduated to Eton, the cradle of English gentry.

Church attendance was part of school life, a formality which one rarely questioned. Religion wasn't something to get excited about, rather it was to be endured. Charles said later in life when reminiscing on his childhood, 'I used to think that religion was a Sunday thing, like one's Sunday clothes, to be put away on Monday morning. We boys were brought up to go to church regularly, but although we had a kind of religion, it didn't amount to much. It was just like having toothache. We were always sorry to have Sunday come, and glad when it was Monday morning. The Sabbath was the dullest day of the whole week, and just because we had got hold of the wrong end of religion.'

An unbelievable shock was just about to hit these three young Etonians; life back at Tedworth House had been thrown into a spin by the whole-hearted conversion of Edward Studd. The gambling racehorse owner had become a red-hot, soul-winning Christian; quite the most embarrassing thing that could happen in his children's lives!

Edward Studd was now fifty-six, his hair greying, but his eyes still looking out direct and clear under the strongly marked eyebrows. Days, weeks, months and years—a lifetime had slipped by, filled out in every corner with a certain satisfaction. Time and energy had been tirelessly devoted to passing pleasures. In the summer it was cricket, cricket practice, cricket matches and cricket weeks—so much so that Dora found the garden sadly neglected because the gardeners were always being called away from their work during the school holidays to bowl or field for the boys.

Then there were the horses to be exercised at exhilarating speed round the course or in the winter the thrill of the hunt. Edward's visits to Tattersalls, the famous horse dealing and betting rendezvous, were so frequent that he purchased a fine London Victorian mansion—2 Hyde Park Gardens—on the north side of the park, to facilitate his pastime. One would have thought that Edward's kind of life, happily divided between country, town, and family was completely insulated from 'the missions', as they were called, that D L Moody, the American evangelist, and Ira D Sankey were holding in many towns and cities of the British Isles. But this was not so.

CHAPTER TWO

A BRAND NEW LIFE

B Y CHANCE, an old friend, Mr Vincent, who had owned a neighbouring plantation in India, found himself stranded in Dublin when he missed the boat back from the the Punchestown races. He had no choice but to return to his hotel, and with a free evening before him he decided to look for a theatre. The first place that caught his attention advertised Moody and Sankey. Not familiar with these names and wondering what kind of act it was, he went in.

It was not long before Mr Vincent realised he had inadvertently walked into a religious meeting. The place was crowded. 'Surely these preachers are popular,' he thought. There on stage stood Sankey singing an old hymn rarely sung today. Without realising why, Mr Vincent hung on every word; he felt most uneasy in these unfamiliar surroundings, but he was riveted to the spot.

As the singer sat down, evangelist D L Moody rose to his feet. After the preaching Mr Vincent watched as a stream of people walked out into the enquiry room. No, that wasn't for him. He turned and joined the jostling crowd as they spilt out onto the pavement.

Strangely, the next day he made no attempt to return home. In the evening he took his place again to hear the preaching. We are not sure how many times he attended but before he left Dublin a life-changing decision had been made.

As the invitation to come to Jesus rang out, compelled by the Spirit of God, he joined the line of those going to the enquiry room. D L Moody, with no time for lengthy counselling, said, 'Mr Vincent, do you believe Jesus Christ died for you?' 'I do,' he replied. 'Then,' said Moody, 'thank him.' He did and left Dublin a transformed man.

As Moody and company travelled, the reports of their activities filled the papers. The largest halls in the land were too small. Rich, poor, young and old alike flooded into the meetings, and they were gripped by Moody's simple preaching of the gospel and the powerful message in song from Sankey.

Moody solved his biggest problem by putting up special halls which seated about 5,000 people. These halls, similar to tents, were taken to congested parts of London and were erected on eleven different sites. Moody spoke two, three, or even four times a day to packed audiences, and altogether over two million people heard him preach.

Obviously such happenings attracted a great deal of press comment, and not all of it was polite. Edward Studd could not have failed to read the reports and was probably slightly amused by these unconventional happenings. At one time he announced, 'I would like to hear this man myself when he comes to London. There must be some good in him.'

Back again in London Mr Vincent pursued his new spiritual life. He frequently visited the Moody-Sankey meetings which had now moved to the Drury Lane Theatre.

About the same time Mr Vincent received a letter from his old friend Edward Studd who was eager to share an item of special news. Edward had purchased a new horse, the best he had ever owned, and now he had entered it for a big race. So certain was he that it would win, he wrote, 'If you are a wise man, come to the race and put every penny you can on my horse.'

The two friends arranged to meet in London when Edward had business to do at Tattersalls. Turning to his friend as they left together he said,

'How much have you put on my horse?'

Mr Vincent replied, 'Nothing.' Edward couldn't believe it.

'Well, you're the biggest fool I ever saw. Didn't I tell you it will win? Never mind—although you're a fool, come and let's have dinner.'

They went to 2 Hyde Park Gardens and dined alone. Edward, in a genial mood, said,

'Where shall we spend the evening? We will go anywhere you suggest.'

'How about Drury Lane?' said Mr Vincent.

'What, but that's the place where those preachers are, and it's not Sunday. Choose a theatre or a concert.'

'Didn't you say it was my choice? Come on, let's go to Drury Lane.'

Edward, a man of his word, consented in a good-natured fashion, but on arriving at the theatre there was plenty to deter them. The place was already full and crowds were milling around outside trying to get in. Scribbling a note quickly on his visiting card Mr Vincent sent a message via a steward to one of the organisers. 'I've got a wealthy sporting friend with me and I'll never get him here again if I don't get seats tonight.'

It worked. The steward returned and beckoned them in by a side door. In a matter of moments they were seated on the front row directly under the nose of D L Moody. Edward fixed his eyes on Moody and never let them stray. Moody's words fixed themselves in Edward's heart so that as they were leaving, he said, 'I will come and hear this man again.'

The conversion of Edward Studd was total. He set himself to follow his Saviour with the same passionate zeal that had driven him for fifty-six years in the pursuit of horses and pleasure. The Christian Edward Studd was the same resolute, outspoken character who not only thought his friend Mr Vincent was a fool but said, 'You're a fool,' when he resisted the temptation to put money on a race horse.

As Edward boldly grasped the implications of his new salvation he didn't flinch from the changes he knew he must make. His single-mindedness wouldn't allow any compromise in his Christian behaviour. He knew he could not continue to live as before so he sought an interview with Mr Moody to settle the issue once and for all. 'Now I am a Christian do I have to give up party-going, racing, shooting, hunting and theatres?' Moody responded with similar forthrightness: 'Racing means betting and betting is gambling; there's no place for that in a Christian life. The other things? You please yourself, but I tell you, once you have won someone else to Jesus Christ you will not be interested in these other things.'

Edward proved the truth of those words. The spiritual revival generated by the Moody-Sankey mission now came like a hurricane to Tedworth House. When a guest remarked that he had heard that Mr Studd had become religious or something, the coachman aptly explained, 'Well sir, we don't know much about that, but all I can say is that though there's the same skin, there's a new man inside!'

Faithfully Edward took the gospel to his relatives, but unfortunately he was no tactician. He charged at each opportunity like a bull at a gate. 'Are you saved? If not you will go to hell and that's flat.' His brother-in-law George received such a blast and none too kindly. The door slammed shut as Edward left, never to be received there again. Herbert, one of the younger sons, accompanied his father to the stables when Edward called out across the lawn to a gardener, 'Giles are you saved?' Indignation and embarrassment filled the young man's heart, and sixty years later, when he recalled the story, the quiver of those emotions welled up in his voice.

Dora must have wondered where it would all end. Edward severed all his racing interests, sold his horses, but kept a hunter for each of his sons. He opened up Tedworth House to the local community, so concerned was he that they too should have an opportunity to hear the gospel. He would ride out around the countryside inviting rich and poor alike to hear preachers he would invite down from London. Moody himself came on one occasion. The furniture in Tedworth Hall was replaced with benches, where row upon row the congregation crammed in, overflowing up the stairs and even leaning over the banisters. Charlie and his brothers were insulated from all these amazing happenings. Life at Eton went on as usual while Edward continued to follow Moody, taking all those he could to hear him.

Edward Studd continued as a zealot to the day of his death, when it was truly said, 'He had accomplished more in his two short years as a Christian than most do in twenty.' Even the manner of his death was a fitting epitaph to this gallant man. One evening on his way to a Moody meeting he suddenly remembered he had forgotten to bring one of his grooms. Telling the coach driver to continue he jumped down and ran all the way back. Unfortunately he damaged a blood vessel in his leg and died. His last activity was selfless service. In life he was a fearless witness who unconsciously set before his sons an incredible standard.

CHAPTER THREE

ETON DAYS

I N 1877, THE YEAR of their father's conversion, Charles with his brothers, was involved in a different kind of excitement. All three boys had the honour of being in the Eton cricket eleven together, the first time such a thing had happened. When they received a letter from their father inviting them to join him in London, their first thought was, 'He will take us to the theatre.' The young men were in for a surprise. Their father now had one driving passion: to see his sons saved. He marched them off to hear Moody. Never in their lives did they conceive of people going to religious meetings except on Sundays, but they had to admit it was interesting.

His sons returned to school and the matter rested there for the time being. When term ended, Charlie, sixteen years old, and his brothers, probably seventeen and eighteen, returned to Wiltshire and Tedworth House. The three brothers were often referred to by their initials. Kynaston, J E K, was the eldest, and George, G B, was followed by Charlie, known as C T. These young men who had never known anything but luxury were welcomed back into the bosom of the family. The house bustled with activity. The younger boys were thrilled to have their big brothers home. They were fun, ready to display their prowess in the saddle or on the cricket pitch to the delight of the youngsters. Dora smiled; she enjoyed her children. What fine young men they were be Home, whether a mansion or a hovel, is ordinary to a child, so I doubt that the grandeur of Tedworth House impressed itself upon young C T Studd. Gradual gentle steps led from the garden to the dignified Greek-style entrance supported by four tall columns. Inside, a smaller hallway opened out into the grand hall where a graceful fan-shaped staircase swept down from a delicate balcony encircling the first floor. The well-proportioned drawing room opened out from the hall. Sunlight flooded in through the long windows as maids busied themselves dusting and sweeping the generous room. The furnishings were expensive and the decor in keeping with the grand houses of that era.

At sixteen years old Charles was probably more concerned to get out and see how many runs he could make than to admire the sweep of the landscape and the beautiful gardens with lawns stretching away from the house—although I trust some of these impressions were stored away as sweet memories.

Some years later C T was telling a group of young people about returning to Tedworth for the holidays and his amazement at the change in his father. 'We couldn't understand what had come over him. He kept telling us that he had been "born again" and at night would come in to my room to talk about my soul. He would ask if I was saved. I got wise and would pretend to be asleep as soon as I heard him coming. Everyone in the house had a dog's life till they got converted. His insistence made us avoid him so that we would quickly move round the other side of the house if we saw him coming.'

A year later Charles and his brothers were home again. Their father continued with his programme of meetings at

Tedworth House, and no doubt with the conversion of his sons in mind, Edward invited two young men to stay for the weekend and to preach on the Sunday evening. Unfortunately one of them, Mr Wetherby, didn't impress these able, talented sons of Edward; the poor man could hardly ride and wasn't much good at cricket either.

Nonetheless Wetherby had his uses. That afternoon he individually brought these three young men to surrender their lives to Christ. C T said in a testimony years later that, 'As I was going out to play cricket he caught me unawares and asked, "Are you a Christian?" I said, "I'm not what you'd call a Christian. I have believed on Jesus Christ since I was knee-high. Of course, I believe in the church too." I thought, by answering him pretty close, I would get rid of him, but he stuck as tight as wax and said, "Look here, God so loved the world that he gave his only begotten Son, that whosoever believeth on him should not perish, but have everlasting life. You believe Jesus Christ died?" "Yes." "You have believed he died for you?" "Yes." "Do you believe the other half of the verse: 'shall have everlasting life?'" "No," I said, "I don't believe that." He said, "Now, don't you see that your state-ment contradicts God? Either God or you is not speaking the truth, for you contradict one another. Which is it? Do you think God is a liar?" "No," I said. "Well, then, aren't you inconsistent, believing one half of a verse and not the other half?" "I suppose I am." "Well," he said, "are you always going to be inconsistent?" "No," I said, "I suppose not always." He said, "Will you be consistent now?" I saw that I was cornered and began to think, if I go out of this room inconsistent I won't carry very much self respect. So I said, yes I would be consistent. "Well, don't you see that eternal life is a gift? When someone gives you a present at Christmas what do you do?" "I'd take it and I'd say thank you." He said, "Will you say thank you to God for this gift?" Then I got down on my knees and I did say thank you to God. And right then and there joy and peace came into my soul. I knew then what it was to be born again, and the Bible, which had been so dry to me before, became everything.'

CT's conversion didn't begin with 'all fire and zeal'; he went back to Eton without even mentioning his step of faith to anyone. Although Mr Wetherby, the young visitor, had had the privilege of leading Charlie to Christ, Charlie knew he owed his conversion to his father's prayers and diligence. Secretly he admired him—his own father was the most real Christian he had ever met.

A few days elapsed and then Dora and Edward received the most thrilling mail. 'Dear Father, I should have told you; when Mr Wetherby came I invited Christ into my life.' C T wasn't alone in writing; his two brothers also put pen to paper and individually confessed their faith in Christ. All the secrets were brought into the open when Edward replied with a joint letter to his sons. Now they all knew the young man was more able than they had thought.

Surely it demands more courage and ability to be a good witness than to shine on the cricket field, a lesson Charlie was to take a few years to learn.

Immediately the three Etonians initiated a bible study which Kynaston led. He proved himself to be a faithful follower of Christ and a consistently good example to his brothers.

Charlie continued to be known as a Christian, but for the most part cricket was his prime passion. Like his father he had a one-track mind. If he was to play cricket, he must do it well. His best hours were given to training and disciplined practice. It wasn't by chance he was reported to be 'incomparably the best cricketer' following the Eton and Harrow match of 1879, the year he was captain.

On leaving school his house master wrote of him, 'Perhaps he might have done more work, but it is hard for the captain of the eleven, and he has done no little good to all who have come under his influence. I think the secret of the charm of his character is that he thinks for others rather than for himself.'

With school days behind him a new phase of life was about to unfold.

CHAPTER FOUR

CAUGHT OUT

I T WAS ALMOST automatic that Eton should lead on to Cambridge and Trinity College. C T Studd's cricketing fame went before him so that he immediately received his blue and for the next four years played for his university. In 1882 he was in the eleven when Cambridge University had an unprecedented victory over the unbeaten Australians in a most exciting match. Overnight the name Studd was on the lips of the nation. All three Studds were in the winning team, and C T excelled himself with a most outstanding innings. Never before had there been three brothers in the same team and all of them first class cricketers. It was Punch which nicknamed them 'the set of Studds'. A certain banker had three gold studs on his evening shirt engraved with the initials of the three brothers. Whoever made the highest score of the day was at the top in his shirt at night. The three brothers created a record at Cambridge which has never been equalled, and each was captain of the eleven in succession.

It is impossible to talk about C T Studd without talking about cricket. It was his all-consuming passion. Through his success on the field he became a national hero. Young and old alike unashamedly praised his magnificent performances and revelled in every report of his brilliance. C T, like any other man, thrived on the national acclaim and loved every minute of it. Newspapers, cricketing journals and influential people all proudly sang his praises. Here was a young Englishman with exceptional ability as batsman, bowler or in the field.

Lillywhites Annual said later that year:

C T Studd must be given the premier position among the batsmen of 1882, and it would be difficult to instance three finer innings played by so young a cricketer against the best bowling of the day, than his three-figure scores against Australia and The Players.

In 1883 C T was accorded, for the second year in succession, the premier position as an all-round cricketer. 'Some years have elapsed since the post has been filled by a player so excellent in all three departments of the game,' reported a cricket commentator of the day. Dr W G Grace, the noted cricketer of that age, said of C T, 'He is the most brilliant member of a well-known cricketing family, and from 1881–1884 had few superiors as an all-round player.'

A cricketing career was inevitable. His brilliance took him to Australia to play for England, and as an excellent all-rounder he was included in numerous other first-class matches.

What was this doing to his spiritual life? A man cannot serve two masters. The Moody and Sankey missions continued throughout Britain to have a powerful spiritual impact upon city after city, but Charlie remained unaffected. Whilst he was enjoying fame with the MCC in Australia, recovering the ashes, Moody came to Cambridge where he conducted an historic mission. Charles' brother Kynaston was chairman of the organising committee. He was the natural choice, a whole-hearted Christian who never shrank from telling his

C T Studd the cricketer. The test team which brought back the 'Ashes' in 1883

Left to right standing—W Barnes, F Morley, C T Studd, G F Vernon, C F H Leslie

Second row—G B Studd, E F S Tylecote, Hon Ivo Bligh (Lord Darnley), A G Steel, W Read Front row—R G Barlow, W Bates fellow students of their need for Christ. Every undergraduate received an invitation to the mission, signed J E K Studd.

When C T returned from Australia he was to be greeted by many changed people in the heightened spiritual atmosphere. Prayer groups met in the various colleges, and some notable young men were talking of becoming missionaries. His brother, in the centre of this religious revival, met daily for prayer in his room with Stanley P Smith. No doubt they prayed for C T, but they could never have dreamt that in a few years he would sail to China with Smith and the 'Cambridge Seven', as they became known. For six years Charles continued in a 'respectable' backslidden state—he lived for cricket instead of Christ.

C T was an immensely popular man. As his house master at Eton had noted, he had a charming character and was thoughtful of others. His big sense of humour and high spirits brought him into the centre of college fun. Good looks, his amazing sporting abilities and his height (six feet) made it impossible for him to be overlooked.

Throughout this period he maintained a low-level spiritual life and said of himself that he wasn't averse to joining in singing 'Sankeys' round the piano or having a 'read and prayer'. Occasionally he attended the daily prayer meeting, and was known to be a Christian, to the extent that he willingly handed out invitations to new undergraduates for the college Christian activities. His college years passed with success and fame, but missed the true purpose for his life. He flitted round the edge of real spiritual demands and never led anyone to Christ. Later he said of those years, 'Instead of going and telling others of the love of Christ, I was selfish and kept the knowledge to myself. The result was that gradually my love began to grow cold and the love of the world began to come in.'

It is surprising how many men and women mightily used

by God testify to a period of vague spirituality. Powerful temptations were dangled before C T Studd. He had wealth and fame, and anything he wanted could be his—but the more powerful One was about to move in. God has his ways and means of reaching every heart and negating the power of temptation.

Just as C T was nearing the end of his exciting Cambridge years, news came that his brother George was desperately ill with pneumonia. C T was closest to his brother in age and affection. Kynaston's uncompromising Christianity had made him something of an austere man, though one to be secretly admired; perhaps this distancing caused C T to develop the stronger relationship with George. Years later, in 1927, Kynaston was made Lord Mayor of London. What an honour for such a true man; God has a variety of ways to reward faithfulness.

Charles made haste to Hyde Park Gardens. Up the familiar stairs to the third floor, he hurried along the corridor to a small bedroom. Heavily curtained windows overlooked the grey street outside. The scene in the bedroom was as tinged with death as the wintry trees outside.

George lay on the high bed with its brass bed knobs. He looked horribly white, and as he breathed his chest made rattling noises. C T was quite devastated by his brother's condition. George was only one year his senior, a fine cricketer who had been in the memorable eleven which defeated the Australians at Cambridge; he too had played for England in the famous team that brought back the ashes. What could be more alive than a fine, healthy, athletic, young man playing for his country—but now? Charlie sat close to the bed and looked into the weary face. What thoughts must have run through his head. 'O God! Life is so fragile—that could be me.'

When the shadow of death hovers it immediately silences all other voices with its pressing demand for attention. It focuses the mind as few other experiences can. Suddenly questions rise which now cry out for urgent answers. No longer can they be pushed aside by the clamour of the world. Answers must be found. What am I doing with my life? What is life all about? Where am I going? Lord, what do you want me to do?

George drifted in and out of sleep, its fuzziness rarely leaving his mind. Despite this his spiritual eye had become clarified during the days of sickness. Spiritual realities stood out in sharp contrast against the world, now lost in a blur. All other interests faded in the light of Jesus his Saviour. Nothing else mattered. His whole fragile life was centred on him and his word.

The nights were long. C T had plenty of time to contemplate. Later in life Charlie shared with his own children the thoughts that had surged through his mind as he sat by his brother's bedside night after night. 'Now what is all that cricketing fame worth? What are riches worth when life hangs in the balance? What's it all worth? Nothing in this world has any worth, any value, when death stares in the face. Life, real life is the one supreme importance. All else is vanity. "Vanity, vanity, all is vanity."'

C T was deeply sobered by this experience. The Holy Spirit, who is so faithful, applied the lessons of George's condition to Charlie's heart in a way that perhaps no one can comprehend. Maybe this was aided by two old ladies, friends of Edward Studd, who had taken it upon themselves to pray for Charlie. Their faithfulness no doubt was partially instrumental in drawing him back again to the Lord.

When he could pull himself away from his brother's bedside, he decided to attend a Moody meeting. It was January 1884 when Moody was in St Pancras, London. The long period spent with his brother had been a means of separating his affections from the pull of this world. In the light of eternal values he had seen for himself the futility of worldly gain, fame and position. As he went into the meeting every-thing came to his spirit with force. The songs brought a tear to his eyes, and the address came to him as if he heard it alone. His heart was softened and vulnerable. The worldliness that had insulated it for so long had gone—he heard the word of God.

C T said simply, 'God brought me back.' He made a new dedication of himself to the Lord. What he had done as a boy was now insufficient for the man. His surrender as a sixteen-year-old had long since been outgrown; that night a new contract was drawn up. 'Lord, everything; all I am and have is yours. My life is only to be lived for you.'

What joy filled his heart! Immediately he was telling others. Suddenly this new life filled his every waking moment and gripped him with a passion to see souls saved. George finally recovered, releasing C T who threw himself into evangelism to the exclusion of everything else. He was irrepressible, busying himself in Christian work and taking as many as he could to hear the evangelist. His final two terms at Cambridge coincided with another visit from Moody. Predictably it wasn't long before he brought his first person to Christ. It filled him with joy. He was the happiest man alive, and for the moment he didn't have to give the future a thought. He said, 'I've tasted most pleasures in life but nothing could compare to this.' Soul winning appealed to something in his spirit—was it coloured by his competitive streak? Once he had the bit between his teeth there was no stopping him. He had found the reason for living; he had discovered the true joy, incomparable to any of the glittering attractions of the world. Fearlessly he witnessed to the under-graduates. With his brother Kynaston he even had the privilege of speaking at subsidiary meetings of the Moody campaign. One of those who responded to Christ was a young student doctor who was later to become Sir William Grenfell, the famous missionary doctor to Labrador.

Soon the cricket season was upon him; was he to play or not? For him the game had lost its appeal; its glamour had faded in the glory of the exciting ministry that had opened up to him. He played a few matches and took the opportunity to invite several of his cricketing friends to hear Moody. He was following his father's technique— 'Get them to hear Moody and they will be saved.' 'Cast your bread upon many waters and in due season it will return to you.' I don't suppose C T thought of that verse when he managed to invite these influential members of the England eleven to Moody's meetings. The season ended in an altogether different kind of triumph for Charles Studd. He saw a number of the team born again, and years later certain ones remembered him daily in prayer when he worked in Africa.

On 19 June, 1884, the Moody campaign ended. Varsity days were behind C T Studd and, with his heart no longer in cricket, he was suddenly asking, 'What do you want me to do, Lord? I only want to serve you.'

CHAPTER FIVE

DECISION TIME

D URING THOSE LAST two terms at Cambridge particular friendships began to influence CT's life. At that point he couldn't have realised the significance of these for the future. Stanley P Smith, a close friend of Kynaston, had left Cambridge and was teaching in Newlands School, south London. One day when Charles met him again in London, Smith was bubbling with joy and couldn't help but tell of the wonderful blessing he had recently received. They walked back to Hyde Park Gardens talking together, and no doubt when Smith left Charlie felt a new challenge.

Some months earlier Stanley P Smith had passed through a spiritual crisis where he had wholly dedicated his life to Christ; but something further had happened to provoke Smith's excited talk that evening. Living in London gave him plenty of opportunity to attend holiness and evangelistic gatherings. At one particular Church Army meeting he had responded to the preaching and openly asked for prayer for the baptism in the Holy Spirit. As he was prayed for he immediately experienced power come upon him, with the result that when he witnessed he did so with an even greater abandonment and zeal. He fearlessly talked to anyone, even in the most unusual circumstances. Smith could not hide his joy. It is not difficult to imagine how disturbing Smith's talk must have been when Studd himself, in a spiritual vacuum, wondered which way to go.

The six months since Charles had rededicated his life to Christ had flown by, packed full with activity. Studd wasn't a man to let the grass grow under his feet. He wanted to do something and do it now! He never deviated from the decision to follow Christ wholeheartedly, even though he felt frustrated and lacked true peace. Now above all he wanted to know what to do with his life, but guidance eluded him. He talked long and hard with many Christian friends; each one gave his advice but it was contradictory. Nothing seemed right to Studd. In his desperation to know the mind of the Lord he got himself into an anxious emotional state. The whole tide of events made him impatient. By the end of June 1884 he was feeling very depressed and restless. Perhaps a contributing factor was that his friends from college days, Smith, Hoste and Cassells, knew exactly what they were doing. Individually they had made the dramatic decision to serve Christ in inland China. But such thoughts had never entered CT's heart.

The situation bore heavily upon him, and he became unwell. It was evident that he needed a complete rest, so he decided to recuperate in the country. For three months he took the opportunity to seek God. Although he avidly read his Bible, unfortunately it proved to be a vain effort in discovering God's will. At the end of his convalescence he returned much better but none the wiser. Time was ticking away, and it seemed the Lord was not speaking to him. Decisions had to be made, so until he received some other clear guidance he agreed that the most sensible plan was to pursue training to become a barrister.

In fact he never did pursue this course of action because

once back in London he felt his decision was wrong. How could he conscientiously take up such a profession when his heart wasn't in it? All he desired to do was serve Christ. Could he spend his days studying and working for his own gain when he had more than enough to live on and millions were going to hell? His heart's desire was to preach Christ and see souls saved.

Although C T could not understand it at the time, this frustrating period in his life was a vital learning experience. It was natural for him to feel that his national standing and personal charisma made him somewhat special. Wasn't he a great asset to the kingdom of God? How could he give up so much and now find himself redundant? Surely somewhere was the perfect ministry for him to slip into. The Holy Spirit was using these perplexing circumstances to accomplish his work in Charles Studd's heart.

At this sensitive time in his life, a tract written by an atheist came into his hands. It read as follows:

If I did firmly believe, as millions say they do, that the knowledge and practice of religion in this life influences destiny in another, religion would mean to me everything. I would cast away earthly enjoyments as dross, earthly cares as follies, and earthly thoughts and feelings as vanity. Religion would be my first waking thought, and my last image before sleep sank me into unconsciousness. I should labour in its cause alone. I would take thought for the morrow of eternity alone. I would esteem one soul gained for heaven worth a life of suffering. Earthly consequences should never stay my hand, nor seal my lips. Earth, its joys and its griefs would occupy no moment of my thoughts. I would strive to look upon eternity alone, and on the immortal souls around me, soon to be everlastingly happy or everlastingly miserable. I would go forth to the world and preach to it in season and out of season, and my text would be, "What shall it profit a man if he gain the whole world and lose his own soul?"

The rather condemning tone of this atheistic tract struck home deeply into C T Studd's heart. He began to review his life in the light of it and decided that his Christian life had been quite inconsistent. This unlikely piece of literature prompted him again to seek God's will. This time he knew it was pointless to ask for other people's opinions; he needed to hear God for himself.

The summer of 1884 was now edging into autumn. Despite C T Studd's earnest seeking, God's will still eluded him. Many sincere Christians could testify to a similar experience. As they sought to know what to do with their lives they found the searchlight of the Spirit turned in upon themselves. It appears at such times that God is not so much interested in what we do, but as to what we are.

All the confusion of the previous months now seemed focused upon one thing. C T Studd found himself in the centre of God's searchlight, and what did it reveal? With painful clarity God gave him a revelation of his own great need of power. God wished to equip his servant before unfolding his plan for him.

Maybe it was the testimony of Stanley P Smith that again sprang to his mind; or was it his own personal reading that brought him to understand the necessity of the baptism in the Holy Spirit with power?

The Lord continued to speak to Charles. The man who had been so full now came seeking to be filled; the one who had been so zealous now felt so needy and longed for the power of the Spirit.

The urgent single-mindedness of Studd in this instance worked in his favour. He would not rest till he knew he had received what God had for him. In childlike faith he believed the Scriptures and received the fullness of the Holy Spirit by faith while praying alone. The expectation of his faith didn't include receiving the gifts of the Holy Spirit; unwittingly conditioned by the theology of his day, he was excluded from

that dimension of spiritual life. During those days the unin-
hibited evangelism of the Salvation Army and the holiness
teaching which they and the Keswick Convention propagated
was the 'new thing'. Those hungry for God crowded into the
meetings where they sought a fresh enduement of the Spirit
by humbling themselves in repentance.

A few days later Charles was invited to a Bible study.
Almost immediately talk centred around a dear lady well
known to those gathered. 'Have you heard of the blessing Mrs
Watson has received?' No doubt the lady was a fine Christian
and had faithfully served Christ for years. Now it was claimed
that despite the many difficulties and troubles in her life, she
had come into a lasting blessing that so filled her with peace
that nothing could move her. It was said, 'She lives a life of
perfect peace.' The group, turning to their Bibles, determined
to see if this blessing could be found in its pages. Before the
evening ended they were on their knees praying for 'the peace
of God, which passeth all understanding' (Phil 4:17) and 'joy
unspeakable' (1 Pet 1:8).

Back home alone in his room C T brought these issues
again before the Lord. He was very earnest and wanted to live
in every blessing God would give him. He had obtained a
book called *The Christian's Secret of a Happy Life* by Hannah
Whitall Smith. Here, laid out plainly, were the steps into a
life filled with the power of God.

Charles Studd read, 'In order to enter into this blessed
interior life of rest and triumph you have two steps to
take—first, entire abandonment, and second, absolute faith.'
Exercised in his spirit, he continued to read and the Lord
began to speak to him. Referring to this experience some
years later he said, 'I discovered that this blessing is exactly
what God gives to everyone who is ready and willing to
receive it. I found the reason why I had not received it was
just this, that I had not made room for it, and I found as I sat
there alone thinking, that I had been keeping back from God

what belonged to him.' He had been bought with a price, the precious blood of Jesus. Painfully he discovered that like a robber, he had robbed God of that which was rightly his. Jesus owned him and yet, Studd said, 'I had kept myself back from him, I had not wholly yielded.' He said, 'When I came to see that Jesus Christ had died for me it didn't seem hard to give up all for him. It seemed just common, ordinary honesty.' On his knees he prayed out from the bottom of his heart the words of Frances Ridley Havergal's hymn:

> Take my life and let it be
> Consecrated Lord to thee.

His abandonment to the Lord was complete. Nothing was held back. In simple faith he believed that what he had given to God, God was well able to keep. 'I realised my life was to be one of simple childlike faith . . . I was to trust in him and he would work in me to do his good pleasure.' From that moment on life was different. The trauma of the previous months evaporated. Peace and joy flooded his heart.

In tracing Studd's spiritual journey we find him again making a full surrender in his life. How can this be? Surely if he had truly abandoned everything to God when he returned from his backsliding there could be no reason for him to be challenged a second time on the same issue? We can only believe that Studd was entirely genuine in his pilgrimage of surrender; he yielded himself to the whole extent of his understanding on each occasion. The Lord was inviting him into a yet closer walk with himself and a greater empowering by the Spirit. Someone has said, 'The gospel is free but it costs you everything.' Studd now found the greater his revelation of the free gospel of grace, the more impelling and costly the invitation to abandon all to Christ and his cause.

Very shortly after this fundamental transaction had taken place the Lord pulled away the veil from C T Studd's future. The way forward began to unfold.

CHAPTER SIX

THE CONFIDENT GENERATION

SO THAT WE CAN better understand some of the powerful influences in C T Studd's life, it would be helpful to paint in the background of the age in which he grew to manhood. Like us all, he was a product of his own generation. His was the Victorian era, with its huge contradictions in society, and a time when the curtain of secrecy, which had veiled the world for so long, was being swept aside. Suddenly no place on earth was too distant to visit, given the will and the courage.

We know he had little time for anything but cricket during his college days, though he could not have avoided hearing the persuasive arguments of the activists and thinkers endeavouring to mould the changing society. Every opportunity was afforded C T to get a 'feel' of his day and age from the many visitors who came to the university, both Christian and secular.

At the point when C T was seeking God's will for his life, Queen Victoria was nearing her Golden Jubilee year. From girlhood to old age she had ruled Britain, leaving her own unique, indelible character upon the nation. Since 1861 she had lived as a recluse, swathed in widow's black. Her austere, forbidding image did little to endear her to the people. Even on state occasions she would not bow to popular opinion; she refused to wear the crown and robes of office, preferring her black bonnet with a touch of white lace. She became an institution rather than a loved person. Although this was so, the normal stable family life that she and Prince Albert enjoyed helped to close a very necessary door upon the debauched lifestyles of her recent forebears. By this she secured a future for the monarchy, in a nation that could so easily have repudiated its royal family and followed in the steps of republican France.

Studd had grown up in the new industrial age with constant change and technical advance transforming the face of England. Although the spiritual life generated by the revivals of the eighteenth century had largely petered out, the repercussions of social change continued.

The nineteenth century is noted for the influential part the philanthropist played in introducing legislation to deal with the gross injustices of society. Generally these activists were a new kind of Christian who appeared on the scene as a direct result of the evangelical awakening that had shaken Britain out of the middle ages. Their efforts began to stir a social conscience in many ordinary people. These big-hearted individuals tackled huge problems which only grew larger and more numerous as the radical change in society gathered momentum.

New industries, like magnets, pulled workers together into factories. Haphazard cities mushroomed around them. The newly-fledged town dwellers had left their rural poverty for a harsher variety. Squalid homes—overcrowded, insanitary hovels—provided their only comfort after long days of toil in equally squalid work places.

Homelessness, poverty and inhumane working conditions, involving women and children also, created a vast subculture. William Booth, the founder of the Salvation Army, called it the 'submerged tenth'—a whole strata of society which was largely unchurched and without Christ.

The concentration of injustice and misery in the towns and cities, especially in the North and the Midlands, fired the reform movements which in Studd's life began to touch every aspect of the nation. Education, conditions of work, protection for women and children, prison reform, sanitation, and extended franchise were all subjects for hot political debate, and right there in the centre were whole-hearted Christians, motivated by the love of Christ, bringing about fundamental changes to the law.

The crying needs of the poor working classes shouted out for justice. Their only power was sheer weight of numbers and the suicidal withdrawal of their labour. In the 1870s and '80s agricultural and industrial depression forced many workers to hunger. Militancy grew and, with the aid of a few sympathetic parliamentarians, trade union legislation was introduced. It was a small beginning but it showed the way for the future.

The visitor to Britain during Victoria's reign would have been most probably filled with enthusiastic praise for the wonderful advances and new technology; the impressive engineering, modern factories, and the wealth of manufactured goods. The Great Exhibition of 1851 was the prototype of the modern World Fair. Under one roof were assembled all the wonders of the new industrial age proudly displayed for the whole world to view.

Truly Britain had much of which to boast. In 1848 she produced half the pig-iron in the world and in the next thirty years managed to treble her output. Her foreign trade was outdistancing that of France, Italy and Germany together. The United States was still in its infancy and not yet a serious competitor. Britain was rich, proud and powerful.

Traditionally the landed gentry had been the wealthy, but now a 'nouveau riche' appeared—the self-made 'gentleman' with money flowing as freely as water in the water mills of the woollen industry.

Alongside these potentially explosive changes, exciting world advances extended the empire till it became that 'on which the sun never sets'. The Victorian age presented much challenge to the young educated gentleman. If his fancy wasn't for industry—and the majority would never have considered it—he could enter politics, which now offered far more real power, or join the army or the foreign service with its endless opportunities for administration and government in the far-flung corners of the British Empire.

The status quo in the universities, especially Oxford and Cambridge, remained untouched. They were like upper-class clubs where the student majority came straight from the public schools.[2] These institutions groomed young men to lead, and prepared them to fill almost any influential public position. Ex-students expected to command the army, stand in Parliament, minister in the Church of England or represent the Queen anywhere in the world. The young man from this tradition who yielded to the demands of the gospel was quickly out in front—leadership was in his blood. He could directly understand the need for missionary enterprise and potentially was well equipped to go.

The empire posed a special opportunity to the Christian. Despite disquiet at home over some of the colonising methods abroad, idealists consoled themselves that western standards of education and Christianity 'would take over the heathen'. Missionaries sometimes preceded the flag, but on many occasions followed where the entrepreneur and trader had already blazed the trail.

In Studd's day world travel was becoming a less unusual activity; he had already made two journeys to Australia to play cricket, and even the working classes, forced by hard times, chanced their luck as emigrants to the United States, Australia or the other new colonies. The world was becoming a smaller place.

Although smaller, it continued to hold hidden wonders and fascination for the traveller. The age of discovery was still alive, when explorers were setting foot upon mountains never before climbed, tracing the sources of rivers and bringing back stories of plants, insects and even large animals never known to the western world. Scientific expeditions were commissioned by the Royal Society to discover the hidden wonders of nature. Anything new demanded investigation and was met with wonder.

For the Christian, their reports held special interest as they spoke of tribes and peoples living their lives in the darkness of superstition and heathen practice. Missionaries, many fired by the same impetus for adventure and themselves great explorers, returned to tell of the plight of those without Christ.

The great missionary movement was at its height. Every new territory that opened challenged fervent Christians. John Paton, ignoring tales of cannibalism, went to the islands of the Pacific. Frequently it was the heroic stories of such courageous men that fired others to go. Many missionary societies had been formed and were sending willing volunteers all over the world. The stories that came back telling of hardships, disease, opposition and so often death, didn't deter others from stepping into their shoes. The need for every man to hear the gospel had become paramount. As men went ahead to open up nations the Spirit of God was there to open up hearts and prepare the way.

Surely C T must have read of the courage and adventures of David Livingstone. Here was a Christian missionary combining the proclamation of the gospel with a fight against disease and slavery, and at the same time taking on a vast task of surveying, mapping and exploration. His purpose: to see the dark continent of Africa opened up to the light of the gospel.

Whilst all these talking points must have engaged the young men at Cambridge for many an hour, it was James Hudson Taylor, the founder of the China Inland Mission, who caused the biggest stir. Here was a man bringing all the idealism of the age to a Christian focus. This intrepid missionary pioneer brought the millions of inland China to the conscience of the church. China needed the gospel and needed it now. China needed missionaries, and no one presented the case more passionately than Hudson Taylor.

The sixteenth, seventeenth and eighteenth centuries had enjoyed significant spiritual movements, but by the 1880s, except for the 1859 revivals in Ireland, nothing had brought hope to England. As spiritual life waned, a battle was being waged to maintain the pure evangelical doctrine. Society was undergoing painful change; all its institutions were open to scrutiny, and almost anybody considered themselves qualified to pass judgement. What happens in the world has a habit of seeping into the church. The age of strident rationalism had arrived.

Most people went to church. It was a time for notable great preachers such as Spurgeon and Bishop Ryle. The church appeared to be making progress; although, as already mentioned, a significant number of the working classes were beyond its reach. These now presented a new missionary challenge. The Salvation Army, formed in 1865, came together with the intention of communicating to these forgotten people.

Sufficient appearance of life marked the church so that the majority took no note of the subtle new enemies sapping away its vitality. Darwinism arrived centre stage and began to shake faith in God's word. It did not take long before German theologians declared that there was no reason why God's word should not be treated like any other book, criticised as to its sources, and, if lacking, corrected as all other books by fallible men. This so-called 'higher criticism' spread in British churches, religious colleges and universities. It began to have a disastrous effect upon evangelical witness, the results of which are still with us. Evangelical truth was fighting for its life.

It was against this background of unbelief, questioning, and formal, respectable religion, that Moody and Sankey arrived at Cambridge University. Moody preached the same basic gospel, stripped of all religious overtones, as when he stood before crowds of working men. It could have appeared crude and offensive except the power of the Holy Spirit was there to convict of sin. Real Christianity was explained to these young men, who for the most part only knew its form. It caught the hearts and imaginations of hundreds, and a movement began that was to lead some of the sons of the famous and wealthy to leave everything and to follow Christ.

Besides the evanglistic thrust of Moody's ministry, his message always came as a challenge to the Christians. They were left in no doubt that they should present themselves wholeheartedly for the winning of others for Christ. He was directly responsible for launching dozens of young men and women into their missionary careers, and C T Studd is numbered among that illustrious group.

CHAPTER SEVEN

THE FLAME IS LIT

L O! I COME SUDDENLY,' is an apt scripture for guidance. For months C T Studd had sought to know God's will, then suddenly—as he totally abandoned himself to God—the way opened. C T Studd said,

I gave myself up to God... From the time I thus trusted him with all my heart, my life has been different. He has given me that peace that passes understanding and that joy which is unspeakable. I had many joys before I gave myself fully to God, but since that time has been the happiest part of my life so far.

So testified Studd at his farewell meeting before sailing to China.

On the 1st of November, 1884, Stanley P Smith, Studd's close friend, returned to London after taking farewell meetings at Oxford and Cambridge. He planned to sail for China with the China Inland Mission in the new year. Kynaston and Charlie were pleased to see him. When they learned he was to attend the farewell meeting of another CIM missionary that evening, Charlie agreed to go.

McCarthy, one of the founder missionaries of the CIM,

told his own story of his call to overseas service twenty years earlier. Charlie said,

> Never shall I forget the earnest and solemn way in which he told us how the Lord had led him to go to China and the need there was there for earnest workers to preach the gospel; how thousands of souls were perishing every day and night without even a knowledge of the Lord Jesus. Then we sang,
>
>> "He leadeth me, he leadeth me,
>> By his own hand he leadeth me,
>> His faithful follower I would be,
>> For by his hand he leadeth me."
>
> I felt he was indeed leading me to go to China, but thought I would not decide at once.

Studd found himself incapable of keeping a secret of such a burning issue. Although he had determined to pray and read the word before taking any action, he blurted it out on the way home while sitting on top of an old-fashioned open top bus. 'I've decided to go to China.' Smith was absolutely delighted.

The enormity of his decision then fell on him like a lead weight. How could he go? It would deeply wound his mother whom he loved so dearly. Taking his Bible from his pocket he read Matthew 10:37: 'He that loveth father or mother more than me is not worthy of me . . .' Strengthened and reassured in his decision, he committed it to God.

First he poured out his embryo plans to Kynaston who deluged them with icy arguments. Then, despite his brother's pleading, he made his proposals known to his mother, who, as he expected, was distraught and heartbroken. The whole family was in a turmoil, crying, pleading and arguing. Even friends and relatives were called to reason with Charlie. Understandably the family doubted the wisdom of his decision; after all, had he not been unwell and far from settled for some months?

His mother pleaded, 'Charlie don't do anything impulsive; leave it for a week or so!' The conflict in those few days was intense. He had expected opposition, but its ferocity battered his emotions. The Studds found it impossible to accept that one of their own should go to be a missionary. Every conceivable attempt was made to hinder or divert him from what they felt was folly. In his family's eyes, to go was to waste a life. Kynaston made one last effort to appeal to reason and said, 'You're making a great mistake. Can't you see you are breaking your mother's heart?'

The two brothers prayed together. C T said, 'I don't want to be pigheaded; I just want to do God's will.' They left it in the Lord's hands and went to bed. Although exhausted, C T found it impossible to sleep. He valued his brother's opinion. Was he making a great mistake?

In the quietness of his own heart the Lord spoke to him plainly and repeatedly, 'Ask of me, and I shall give thee the heathen for thine inheritance, and the uttermost parts of the earth for thy possession' (Ps 2:8).

Never one to delay over decisions, the following day, the 4th of November, C T set off to meet Hudson Taylor, the founder and leader of the mission, who was back in London. Charles, resolute in spirit, had determined to see him; although to do so in defiance of his mother's entreaties was painful to him. The issue was quickly settled. Hudson Taylor gladly accepted him.

The agony of conflict was not so quickly resolved. One evening, waiting for the Bayswater train, his mind was assailed with doubts and visions of his weeping mother. He took out his Bible and read, 'And a man's foes shall be they of his own household' (Mt 10:36). Without condemning his dear mother, the powerful word of God came to his aid again and put strength into him. He knew he had heard from God, and despite the tearing pain in his heart, he would obey.

Every action of faith culminates in a crisis, where all appears lost, hopeless, impossible or even wrong. How we behave at that time determines the future. Do we trust and go through, or do we succumb to anguish and fear? The eye of faith sees past the present difficulties and suffering, and obeys. There is never a way round a crisis that God wishes to use in our lives; the way is through. God designs it to temper the steel of our spirits. So it was for C T. The trial had been tough and not without reason, for the victory promised devastation in the strongholds of darkness.

A whirlwind of events suddenly overtook Studd. Now accepted as an associate missionary with the CIM and expecting to sail for China in the new year, every day was filled with meetings, farewells and exhortations to other young men to wholly follow the Lord.

He travelled to Oxford with Smith and Hoste, another long-standing college friend. The news of Studd's sudden decision to go to China caused quite a stir; the Oxford undergraduates crowded to hear him. The young men stayed for six days and were joined by yet another college friend, Beauchamp, who had decided, following Studd, to volunteer for China.

Smith and Studd travelled on to Cambridge where the fires of enthusiasm had already been lit by Smith's previous visit. A week's mission was planned, and Hudson Taylor joined them. Cambridge had never seen such missionary meetings. The testimonies of these two fine young men—Smith, the stroke of the Cambridge boat, and especially that of Studd who, at the height of his cricketing fame was to leave for China—had a profound impact. After Hudson Taylor's message the invitation was given for those who would serve as missionaries, and forty-five young men filed to the front. Such scenes were unprecedented. The following evening the two conducted a final meeting and another twenty men offered themselves for the mission field, besides many being converted. The colleges were buzzing, and the challenge of Christ became the talk of the day.

Studd's forthright testimony in down-to-earth language, and the fervour of his heart, won the young men. Where he lacked in polished preaching he excelled in communication. The students met the man and knew him to be genuine. Smith and Studd bubbled with joy.

As the men listened to these "spiritual millionaires", as one undergraduate described them, the very context of the word "sacrifice" seemed reversed, and each man wondered whether he could afford the cost, not of utter devotion and worldly loss, but of compromise and the loss of spiritual power and joy.

Nothing less than the experience of these two men was worth having.

Studd not only impressed the undergraduates but also the saintly Handley Moule who was present at these remarkable meetings. One afternoon Moule, a most perceptive man, took Studd for a walk, and afterwards wrote, 'I found Studd's spirit blessed and his experience remarkable.'

In Leicester, during a week of meetings, hours were devoted to prayer, including one whole night. The lives of some, destined to be very influential in the kingdom of God, were transformed during those powerful days. The Rev F B Meyer, a Baptist minister who blessed countless Christians through his ministry and books, wrote,

The visit of Smith and Studd to Melbourne Hall will always mark an epoch in my own life. Before then my Christian life had been spasmodic and fitful...I saw that these young men had something which I had not, but which was within them a constant source of rest, strength and joy. Never shall I forget a scene at 7.00 am in the grey November morning, as daylight was flickering into the bedroom revealing the figures of the devoted Bible students . . . The talk we held then was one of the formative influences of my life. Why could I not do what they had done? Why should I not yield my whole nature to God?

There was nothing new in what they told me. A man must not only believe in Christ for final salvation, but must trust him for victory over every sin and for deliverance from every care. The Lord Jesus was willing to abide in the heart which was wholly yielded to him. . . They urged me to take a definite step and I shall ever be thankful that they did.

A new fire touched F B Meyer's heart and quickened all he did from that day forward.

*　　　*　　　*

Within a matter of a few weeks Studd's life had turned a complete somersault. The frustration and endless seeking were gone. Now he knew where his future lay. He had never known such peace and irrepressible joy. Life was bursting with purpose.

Again, Studd was national news. The report ran, 'Extraordinary interest aroused by the announcement that the captain of the Cambridge eleven and the stroke oar of the Cambridge boat were going out as missionaries.' Their decision gripped the imagination of the ordinary man. Both the secular and religious press carried enthusiastic articles.

Within days the CIM headquarters were receiving invitations from churches, fellowship groups and universities for the young men Smith and Studd. Their ministry, especially in the colleges, was having exceptional results, so that when Reginald Radcliffe, an evangelist friend of Hudson Taylor, arranged for them to visit Scotland, Hudson Taylor reexamined his timetable. What was the Lord saying? Farewell meetings were planned for London. Should the young men delay their departure so as to fully respond to what the Holy Spirit was doing? Every reported blessing that poured into CIM headquarters only released more praise to God and assured Taylor that something unusual was happening. Men being saved and Christians totally yielding to God could only bring glory to Jesus and further the cause of missions world-wide. Mr Taylor could plainly see the way the Spirit was guiding. He went ahead with his London farewell meeting for himself and some other returning missionaries, but released Smith to travel north with Studd for a Scottish tour.

On November 28th, only twenty-eight days after C T had decided to go to China, he was on the night train for Glasgow with nothing but the clothes he stood up in. The mundane, routine things of life completely passed him by. His mother was very distressed:

> I cannot understand my son Charlie's erratic movements and going to Scotland without any clothes of any sort except those he had on. How or why he should wear one shirt night and day till the 9th December is a mystery to me when he has a supply provided, and one has always been taught that cleanliness is next to godliness.

She went on to urge Taylor to place him, when in China, with an older and sober-minded Christian in steady work. 'I feel that he and Mr Stanley are too much of the same impulsive nature and one excites the other.'

The Scottish venture saw them breaking new ground; they approached the ministry with no confidence in themselves or their past successes. They spent all the afternoon on their faces pleading with God to come down and give them the victory.

Despite fears that no one would turn up for the meetings, they were packed and powerful from the outset, quite unlike any previous Christian gatherings. As the two missionaries entered the hall they were warmly cheered. Studd was the first one to speak, but it was reported, 'He couldn't speak a bit. It was the fact of his devotion to Christ which told and he, if anything, made the greatest impression. Again and again he was cheered. The fact that a man with such prospects as he should thus devote himself, and his fortune, gave them as interest in him from the very first,' wrote the chairman. In an age of ponderous homilies, by very contrast, Studd's happy ungarnished story of his spiritual development held the students spellbound.

I'm sure CT's anxious mother was comforted a little to read Charlie's letter that told of 'much power, many souls saved, remarkable meetings with the students,' and spoke of a time when 'God came down mightily.' On another occasion he wrote, 'We had a huge after-meeting, it was like a charge of dynamite exploding among them.'

The two 'athlete missionaries', as they were called, moved on to Edinburgh University. In the face of spiritual hostility the great hall filled and the students heard them gladly. The reserved gentlemen organisers had been a little shocked by Studd's manner of praying when he had thanked the Lord for the victories God *would* accomplish that evening. His prayer of faith was vindicated.

> No sooner had the benediction been pronounced than there was a stampede to the platform, nor was it mere curiosity. They were crowding round Studd and Smith to hear more about Christ— deep earnestness was written on the faces of many . . . it was all so evidently the work of the Holy Spirit.

Later that night, at the station, hundreds of students fêted them like conquering heroes, calling for them to return and wishing them God's speed.

The spiritual upheaval almost caused a day-by-day alteration to Hudson Taylor's plans. His group of recruits were growing: Hoste, Cassells, Smith and Studd were now joined by Montague Beauchamp, whose sister had just married Kynaston Studd. Then a few days after Christmas, the two brothers, Cecil and Arthur Polhill-Turner, made the group up to seven. Immediately they were dubbed the 'Cambridge Seven'. They became famous; even Queen Victoria accepted a booklet of their testimonies.

Studd continued to busy himself with meetings from Brighton to Liverpool. Then on January 8th, for the first time, all seven were together on the platform of Exeter Hall for Hudson Taylor's final farewell meeting. From that time on the 'Cambridge Seven' became a household name.

The call back to Edinburgh was heard as the call of God, and the next day Smith and Studd were again heading north. The organising committee, now stronger in faith, took the largest hall in the city and the pre-prayer meeting interceded for over one hour.

Charlie gave his testimony 'in quiet but intense and burning utterances, to the love and power of a personal Saviour.' Smith again preached the gospel 'stretching out his long arms in entreaty while he eloquently told out the old story of redeeming love.'

Reginald Radcliffe rejoiced to see the harvest of souls. Even the following day a succession of students called upon them wishing to yield their lives to Christ. Interviews had to be restricted to only a quarter of an hour when Studd would ask, 'Are you a Christian?' 'No,' 'Would you like to be one?' 'Yes.' And so they would pray.

The final gathering was perhaps the most remarkable. Three or four hundred stayed to an after-meeting, and midnight came before they finished helping those seeking God. A cable to Hudson Taylor on his way back to China said, 'Glory to God, three thousand in the meeting tonight.'

They moved on through a number of northern towns. What they *were* gave them a unique appeal. Crowds came wherever they went, and countless souls were born into the kingdom of God.

Charles wrote to his mother,

I cannot tell you how very much the Lord has blessed us. We daily grow in the knowledge of Jesus and his wonderful love; what a different life from my former one. Why, cricket and rackets and shooting are nothing to this overwhelming joy. . . . I am finding out so much more about the poor in the great towns. It has increased my horror at the luxurious way I have been living; so many suits and clothes of all sorts, whilst thousands are starving and perishing of cold, so all must be sold when I come home if they've not been so before.

What do we learn of Studd in this most exciting and impressionable period of his life? We see the beginnings of his discomfort about his riches. Both Smith and Studd—from similar backgrounds—reacted violently to the comfort of their former lives. 'C T believed in rigid austerity,' wrote Cecil Polhill, later describing a journey in China, 'and no comfort of any sort, either of furniture or luxury in food, were for a moment allowed. He would not allow himself even a back to a chair.'

We see too that he had an ability to communicate, although he did not possess the eloquence of Smith. His gift excelled in the sharp thrust of burning words or in the quick turn of humour.

His brusque manner hid a great gentleness of heart, which was revealed again and again in his dealings with those seeking God. His final words of testimony before sailing for China still ring with their original urgency and have not lost their importance: 'God does not deal with you until you are wholly given up to him, and then he will tell you what he would have you do.'

How many good Christian people are tossing around wondering what God would have them to do? Isn't the answer here? God doesn't change his ways—he waits and waits till we are wholly given to him. C T made two or three attempts before the transaction was complete. Can I encourage you, with the example of C T, not to give up?

Come again to the Lord. Or can I draw you to look again at F B Meyer who was thirty-seven years old when he met twenty-four-year-old C T Studd? It was not too late for this servant of God to make a definite, detailed commitment of every area of his life. Today we still live off the fruits of that obedience.

Impassioned words closed the final meeting: 'What are you really living for? Are you living for today or are you living for the eternal life? Are you going to care for the opinion of men here, or the opinion of God? The opinion of men will not avail us much when we get before the judgement throne, but the opinion of God will. Had we not then better take his word and implicitly obey it?' An exhortation rang out: 'Extend your hearts and go out into all the world. Unless we spread abroad the light we find in England we cannot hold our own with the powers of darkness.' Hugh Price-Hughes closed the meeting. As the audience rose he said, 'There is enough power in this meeting to stir not only London and England but the whole world.'

CHAPTER EIGHT

THE CHINESE
TRAINING SCHOOL

ON FEBRUARY 5TH, 1885, a crowd of loving friends and tearful relatives huddled round a carriage door at Victoria Station in London. The Cambridge Seven were leaving. This aristocratic, athletic and influential group of young men would soon be in China. They had made surrender to Christ a popular talking point and, in an unusual way, broken through the formality of their class to communicate in man-to-man terms with ordinary people.

Lady Beauchamp, Kynaston Studd and his new wife were to accompany them as far as Calais. Studd's popularity had drawn several of the MCC team there to make their final farewells. Punctually the train drew out of the station. The Cambridge Seven wistfully watched as they sped past the green fields of England, and with them went a way of living that they would never again enjoy.

C T wrote copiously to his mother giving her great detail of their fascinating journey. Once on board ship 'the seven' began to evangelise their captive congregation of passengers and crew. C T said,

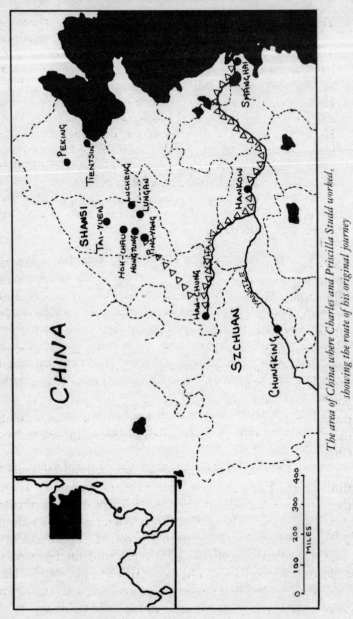

The area of China where Charles and Priscilla Studd worked, showing the route of his original journey

There are seven second class passengers, and we trust that all are now God's own children. The case of one is truly marvellous. The man is a captain of an Indian steamer and had been noted for lying, drunkenness, swearing and blasphemy. Well thank God, he has brought even this man to know Jesus as his Saviour. Hoste began to talk to him the first day, then somehow, one afternoon the Lord led me to go and speak to him about his soul. He seemed softened and I urged him to decide at once. On his knees in his cabin, he received the Lord Jesus. He has three times publicly given his testimony. His whole life has changed. Most of the day is taken up with reading the Bible. Praise the Lord! It is lovely. Not only have these been brought to the Lord but also several of the stewards. You can imagine what a change that means among the ship's company.

As the ship proceeded via Brindisi, Suez, Alexandria, Colombo, Penang, Singapore and Hong Kong, it left a trail of blessings. When in port, the enthusiastic new missionaries went ashore and preached wherever they could. Many weary soldiers of Christ were encouraged and people saved.

Overflowing with joy, Studd wrote, 'The captain gave us permission to hold a service on the quarter-deck; nearly all the passengers came including the first and second class.' The young men preached the same unadulterated gospel and pulled no punches before the worldly and the church-going upper classes. Openly they invited people to respond to Christ.

Instead of sunning themselves in deckchairs as they passed through the Red Sea, they planned periods of study where they began to battle with the Chinese characters. Eventually the ship docked in Shanghai and C T wrote, 'Dear Hudson Taylor came down to the river to meet us.' Immediately a series of special meetings were arranged for the purpose of making a spiritual impact upon the British community. The Temperance Hall, the largest venue in town, was booked for March 23rd, and there the meetings reached a climax.

Among the speakers was C T Studd who again, in his own powerful, provoking manner, told his story. The Rev Fred Smith, the British chaplain in charge of the cathedral in Shanghai, 'stood forward at the end of the meeting and gave a most forthright testimony'. He humbly confessed that if he had been called away the night before he would have been a lost soul, but now he stood there by the grace of God. Brought up by pious parents and well instructed in the Bible, then confirmed and ordained in the Church of England, with the best intention of serving Christ, he had striven as hard as a man could, but had not committed his own soul to the Saviour. Now he said with confidence, 'I am the Lord's and he is mine.'

Studd and the Polhill-Turners (a little later they dropped Turner from their name) had entered China as associated missionaries with CIM. Understandably, the mission had barely had time to decide about the Polhill brothers — they had only applied on January 8th — but Studd was possibly an associate because he chose to be self-supporting. In all accounts of their activities no distinction is made between them and their friends, who were accepted as probationary missionaries.

Mission policy decreed that all working in inland China should wear national dress. For the men this meant not only abandoning trousers and shirts for Chinese-style skirts and long sleeved gowns, but shaving their heads and wearing pigtails!

Before leaving Shanghai they had a hilarious morning experimenting. C T said, 'I have been laughing all day at our grotesque appearance.' Laughter was soon to be replaced by the trials of travel and the particular pressures of adjusting to a new land.

The Seven had enjoyed their months of fellowship. The rich days together had influenced them all in a variety of ways, but now it was soon to end. On April 4th, Studd and

The Cambridge Seven—C T Studd, M Beauchamp, S P Smith,
A T Polhill-Turner, D E Hoste, C H Polhill-Turner, W W Cassels

the two Polhills left for Han-chung in the north, and the others were scattered far afield in inland China.

First they sailed up the Yangtze to Hankow, 700 miles in four days by steamer. Then they continued up the River Han to Han-chung by river boat. The distance was 1,100 miles, and it took them four months. Studd wrote, 'We had grand times together the three of us all day long reading the word and praying. Then the last month Mr Parker came and took charge of the other boat and joined heart and soul with us. It was a grand time and the Lord taught us many things.' Not the least of them was Chinese; to assist them in their study an excellent teacher travelled with them.

Every day presented plenty of first-hand opportunity for the travellers to accustom themselves to Chinese life. There was only one way of living and that was Chinese style. Too soon they learned about cramped quarters, discomfort, flies, rats, noise, smells, heat, filth and cruelty. They were constantly under scrutiny from prying eyes; their every activity was closely watched. Never had such an interesting spectacle passed that way before. They were to discover that, when constantly stared at, it took a lot of grace to be good-natured.

All day long and well into the night the singsong sound of Chinese pounded their ears. How they longed to be able to communicate. There were so many people, all without Christ, but Studd and the two brothers felt gagged. The language seemed so difficult. Hours were spent with their teacher, but they could barely measure their progress.

The initial months in China caused Studd much soul-searching. His inability to communicate gave a golden opportunity to delve deeper and deeper into the word of God. While removed from the limelight of preaching and the thrill of the work, God was refining his servant. Constantly he spoke to him about being dead to himself.

On August 22nd, on his arrival at Han-chung, Studd wrote a letter:

> I have come through many trials and the Lord has taught me many lessons, especially out of my own weakness. How my best powers and attainments can hinder him, that if I live and do, I must be a hindrance to his working through me. Yes, I must be dead, then he can use me for his glory (Gal 2:20). Yes, dead, dead, dead—dead to everything, to everybody, to the opinions not only of the world but also of the Christian world. Peter was not dead to the opinions of his fellows and he fell and was rebuked by Paul. This latter lesson is the special one that the Lord has been teaching me.

Was Studd baulking at the discipline of the mission and mistakenly considering it necessary to be dead to their opinions? Studd fell into a cunning deception of the devil. Like any enthusiastic young Christian he was a target for superspirituality. Hudson Taylor wrote,

I am so sorry that Studd and the Polhill party have taken up such extreme views. They have a good teacher and helpful friends, but have given up study and are asking for the language miraculously by fasting and prayer! How many and subtle are the devices of Satan to keep the Chinese ignorant of the gospel.

After further correspondence Hudson Taylor wrote, in October 1885, 'Charles Studd and the others have restarted language study and seen through some of their mistakes.'

Understandably the new missionaries were very frustrated. Hadn't they seen dozens, even hundreds, coming to Christ before they left home—and now? It was easy to fall into the trap of criticising the mission's methods, and while having no experience of the situation, to consider that perhaps they knew better. Familiar? I'm afraid even some of those most mightily used by God can feel quite ashamed by their past ignorant, arrogant, childish ways.

The early months of CT's time in China were spent in endless long journeys. He was soon to discover that boat travel was luxury compared to the painful grind of walking forty miles a day over mountain and plain in footwear that fitted only approximately. The pitiless sun beat upon the small party as they attempted to be athletic in clothes better suited to sleeping. The quarters the three men had shared on the boat had been comfort indeed compared to the scruffy hospitality received each night in village inns, where they slept on the communal board.

Charlie's desire to serve the Lord sprang from the deepest sincerity. Although these early days in China were anything but easy, he yielded to the Lord and wanted to learn all he could from his new experiences. The CIM was characterised by the martyr spirit clearly expressed in its founder and leader, Hudson Taylor, but seen in countless nobodies who laid down their lives to see China saved. Frequently C T Studd's path led to a haven where he met one of these 'ministering angels'. The standard of devotion to Christ and death to self that he saw in so many of his colleagues brought a sympathetic echo from his own heart. Now deep affirmations of his own devotion and will to serve the Lord flowed out in prayer. Even though Charles wasn't leading dozens of people to Christ, a fruitfulness of a different nature was being birthed.

He had a struggle with the Chinese dress, especially in obtaining shoes to fit his very large feet. The first shoemaker engaged fled from the house, utterly refusing to undertake such a gigantic operation! His huge feet were a great joke amongst the people who would often point and have a good laugh at him in the streets. The Chinese generally are small and so are their feet: the tall C T Studd obviously made a very ungainly Chinaman.

C T established a pattern of spiritual life that was to be a source of strength to him for the rest of his days. Early morning, regardless of the hour that they were to set out, he would rise to read and pray. He wrote, 'We slept very comfortably on bare boards it being hot. Up at 2.00 am to have a read with a candle. Got everything ready at 3.30 to start at 4.00.' Interestingly, his father also was a man who required very little sleep. It is reported that at the most unearthly hours, even at two and three in the morning, he would be wandering about looking for someone to talk to. Mercilessly he would shake his victim awake, sitting on his bed shouting, 'Wake up you lazy beggar!' When converted I should think he found a better way to occupy himself.

Writing from Ping-yang in February 1886, C T commented,

The Lord is so good and always gives me a large dose of spiritual champagne every morning which braces me up for the day and night. Of late I've had such glorious times. I generally wake about 3.30 am and feel wide awake, so have a good read, etc, and then an hour's sleep or so before finally getting up. I find what I read then is stamped indelibly upon my mind all through the day; and it is the very quietest of times, not a foot astir, nor a sound to be heard saving that of God. If I miss this time I feel like Samson shorn of his hair and so of all his strength. I see more and more how much I have to learn of the Lord. I want to be a workman approved, not just with a pass degree as it were. Oh I wish I had devoted my early life, my whole life, to God and his word. How much have I lost by those years of self-pleasing and running after this world's honours and pleasures.

Consistently throughout his life he rose early and spent hours in reading the Bible. He learned the art of meditating on God's word which put substance into his prayers of faith. The word provided him with the spiritual resources to claim his inheritance in Christ and live in the bounty of his promises. Later it equipped him so that not only could he give a good testimony, but with a unique flair he preached the word of God.

Every tissue of luxury and comfort was peeled away from Studd, and then he experienced a time which called for endurance in physical suffering. He was to travel northwards to meet Hudson Taylor, when his feet became very sore at the outset of the journey which would take weeks.

Next day my feet were so bad that I had to leave the boots off and take to sandals; but my skin, not being made of leather like the coolies', the straw and string played havoc with me, and at each step cut deeper. It was not all sugar for the thirty miles that day! Next day was of course worse, and after I had gone twelve miles I had to take off the sandals and go barefoot. When I got in, my feet were in an awful state, seven raw places on two feet; but, praise the Lord, it did make one appreciate one's rest in getting in.

He went on to say,

We generally walk eight miles before having breakfast, then we stop at an open shop or rather Chinese restaurant, a hovel with tables and forms and the cooking place, at which we get some rice. Oh we do enjoy our meals on the road. I am now quite a Chinaman and enjoying rice immensely; in fact I prefer the Chinese to the foreign food.

On Saturday my companions, two colporteurs anxious to do the journey quickly, were bent on doing forty miles. This was not a bright outlook for me with my feet. They wanted to get me a horse but could not. So bad were my feet that it seemed an impossiblity to do such a distance; but the Lord did enable me, how I do not know; I know it was very painful indeed, and of course my feet got worse. Next day thirty-eight miles, euh! Each step was like a knife going into them, but I never felt the Lord's presence nearer the whole time. I was mostly alone, especially the last day as I could not keep up with the others. But I do thank God for it all, for he has taught me so many, many lessons by this suffering. One simply felt bursting with praise and wonder at how the Lord had enabled one to get there at all.

Writing again, he concluded the tale:

I know you'll be anxious to hear how my foot is, so I'll tell you how it got better. Though I rested it, it would not heal, but got very puffy and discharged a good deal. So I asked Hogg, a colleague, to anoint me with oil in the name of the Lord Jesus (James 5:14–15) as I believed the Lord would heal my foot. He hesitated at first, but we read James 5 together and prayed. Since then my foot has got most rapidly better. Next day in faith I took it as being well (though it looked anything but so), and walked a good deal on it. It was much less swollen at night. I continued to do nearly twenty miles a day on it since, with the result that it has lost all swelling and is as fine as the sound one and there is no discharge. I do praise the Lord for this.

An experience of suffering was turned into a lesson of faith. On November 3rd, such a short time after his feet had healed, Charlie wrote again to his mother,

> We have just been having a talk over Chinese hardships and we want to know where they are, for we cannot find them and they are a myth. This is far the best life, so healthy and good, lots to eat, drink and good, hard, healthy beds, fine fresh air; and what else does a man want?

By February 1886 Studd had moved on and had the joy of meeting up again with Hoste who commented, 'C T is getting on very fast with the language and will soon make up for the time lost.' It seems Charles, the Polhills and Stanley Smith were all beginning to settle down, learn the language and adjust to the life.

Whilst in Ping-yang Charles wrote to the Christian students at Edinburgh telling them of the joy of meeting Stanley Smith after six months of separation. His words were full of fire and encouragment.

> Impossibilities have no real place in the real Christian's vocabularly. We only know that all things are possible. Some of us have only the jawbone of an ass; but oh, what a mighty weapon that is when surrendered to the Lord Jesus! It beats a whole battery of scientific artillery whose management is kept in human hands . . . . I'm more sure than ever, since coming to China, that the reason why so many Christians get dead and cold is that they refuse to obey Paul's command to rejoice in the Lord always. I'm sure the devil is always trying to keep one from rejoicing in Jesus and especially here in China. I realise now, more than ever, that the joy of the Lord is our strength. Here one finds that the temptations are far stronger and more subtle than at home. You see this is the devil's stronghold, but praise God it won't be for long.
>
> . . . Stanley Smith can speak Chinese pretty well. He took the

meeting last Sunday and the Lord spoke through him for half-an-hour, praise God.

If China is to be turned upside down, the missionaries must be turned inside out first. Pray that the Lord will rouse us all to go forth in his might, conquering and to conquer. Pray that Paul-like men may be raised up. We want the pick of the Christian army here where the devil's headquarters and main army are. Let us all be very, very ambitious for the honour and glory of the Lord Jesus. Your loving brother C T Studd.

A year had passed and, 'All the Cambridge men were getting on well,' it was reported; but Charles failed to become closely knit with the CIM. Whilst the others were regularly corresponding and being published in the mission magazine, he remained uncommunicative. A report to Hudson Taylor says, 'News of the Cambridge men, but not of C T Studd.'

In May of the same year, the Polhill brothers signed the

P C Smith with Priscilla and Charles and their daughter

Principles and Practice of the Mission and were accepted as full CIM probationers. C T was still listed as an associate and continued to be so till 1890, somehow finding himself unable to wholly align with the mission. His independence made him seek a freer, more individual way of working.

In July all the missionaries converged upon Shansi for their annual conference. The programme was abruptly postponed when Mr Adamson of the Bible Society, who was giving hospitality to Studd and Cassells, suddenly became very sick. Studd wrote,

> Of course dear old Cassells and I were most ambitious to nurse him, but eventually with difficulty I gained the day and Cassells went off to another house. The next day it was found out not to be typhus but smallpox. Then Monty put in a claim to nurse him, but you can imagine I was indignant and refused to budge, however it was thought better that another should come to help, so Monty joined me.

The experience of these fearless soldiers of Christ seemed to be a catalogue of trials and sufferings. Again and again they courageously risked their lives for one another in selfless devotion.

The two young men had a crash course in nursing and how to deal with unco-operative servants! Studd learned to die to another area of self-life as he denied his own natural sensitivities and served a very ill man.

After nursing the smallpox victim, he travelled with Hudson Taylor as far as Han-chung. There they received news of riots in Chungking, which sent a shiver down everybody's spine, with visions of senseless murder, looting and burning. No foreigner was safe, and even sympathetic Chinese would fear to give 'foreign devils' protection as reprisals were merciless. Mr Taylor, concerned for the missionaries there, sent two volunteers, Studd and a companion, to see if they could rescue them. When they arrived in the city only the consul remained and he feared to keep the two travellers, but later agreed Studd should stay. Charles said, 'I didn't know until some time after why God had sent me to that place.'

CHAPTER NINE

WHAT IS THIS WASTE?

W HEN C T STUDD'S father had died, his por-
tion of the inheritance was held in trust till he
reached the age of twenty-five. Knowing that
a large sum of money was to be his, Charles
talked to Hudson Taylor before he left England of his desire
to give it all away into the work of God. The Lord had
personally spoken to him from the scripture of the rich young
ruler. Hudson Taylor's wise counsel left him to pray and act
accordingly when the time came.

When C T was making his way through many dangers to
reach Chungking, thoughts of finance never entered his head,
but while staying in the consul's house the Lord drew his
attention again to the story of the rich young man in Scripture. Immediately Charles' mind went back to the vows he
had made to the Lord and his conversation with Hudson
Taylor. Quietly the Lord spoke to him, and he brought his
past declarations fresh to mind. Charles said, 'God made me
just ordinarily honest and told me what to do.'

A few days later letters came from his bankers and solicitor
informing him of his inheritance. The timing of their arrival
was quite amazing, especially as the mail only came twice a

month, and had followed Studd around an area of civil unrest.

C T had just celebrated his twenty-fifth birthday, so suddenly his immobilisation in the consul's house became very relevant. He discovered that to give away his money he required the signature of a government officer on the papers granting the power of attorney.

When Studd had satisfied himself that he knew the mind of the Lord, he asked the consul, Mr Bourne, to witness his signature so as to begin the process of giving away his money. At first Mr Bourne refused, wondering if this was some folly, but when he saw Studd's serious intent he asked him to wait two weeks so that he should have the opportunity to reconsider his decision. At the later date his sober attitude convinced the consul and the papers were duly signed. With no more emotion than writing cheques for his stockbroker, he gave his money away.

At first it seemed the gross value of his inheritance would be about £29,000. In 1987 values it would possibly be worth three million pounds.

He decided that he would begin by donating four lump sums of £5,000 to certain individuals. These gifts give us an insight into his heart affinity with different aspects of the work of Christ. First of all he sent £5,000 to Mr D L Moody requesting him to open a work in Tirhoot, North India—the area where his father owned plantations which produced his fortune. Was Studd trying to pay back a debt? Did he feel a special sense of responsibility to those people dying without Christ who indirectly had provided him with wealth? Perhaps his generosity overflowed to India because he knew it would have been his father's desire if he had lived a little longer. Whatever the motive, we see that Studd felt a certain kindred spirit with India. Years later he went to serve the Lord there. Moody, unable to comply with Studd's request, used the money for the Moody Bible Institute which continues to train and send missionaries worldwide.

The next gift went to George Müller, who had established in Bristol, England, the most impressive work of faith, where he housed and cared for 2,000 orphans by trusting God alone for all their daily needs. As a principle of his faith Müller never let his needs be known to anyone. He taught how to receive from God through prayer alone, and practised it for the large and small needs of the work. The testimony of this man inspired Studd to do likewise. He was excited to have the opportunity to follow his example. He sent him £4,000 to distribute to missions and £1,000 for the care of orphans.

The next gift of £5,000 was to a certain Mr Holland for his work among the poor in London, an expression of CT's compassion for the needy. In the few months before he left England, when he moved out of his cushioned, wealthy circle into the ministry among ordinary people, he had been shocked at the poverty and degradation of his own countrymen.

The last £5,000 went to the work of the Salvation Army in India. This generosity funded a whole new group of workers who, as always, went among the poor. C T Studd repeatedly expressed a great empathy with the Salvation Army. He liked their warlike ways, their work amongst the poor, their militant songs, street marches and bands.

He then wrote five £1,000 cheques: the first for General Booth of the Salvation Army; three to men preaching the gospel and alleviating suffering among the poor and underprivileged in London and Dublin; and one to Dr Barnardo, for his children's homes. When he had dispatched £25,000 around the world, a few thousands were left, much of which he gave to the CIM.

C T Studd had given his money as a simple, calm response of obedience to God's word in his heart. He believed God would provide for him like Müller, so as an act of faith, he transferred his money from the world's banking system to the

Bank of Heaven. Because he believed, 'Give, and it will be given to you. A good measure, pressed down, shaken together and running over, will be poured into your lap' (Lk 6:38, NIV), he expected heaven's interest—one-hundred-per-cent.

When his financial affairs were eventually settled, C T Studd had £3,400 remaining. Soon after these events he met his future wife. Studd had taken note of the injunction, 'But if any provide not for his own, and especially for those of his own house, he hath denied the faith, and is worse than an infidel' (1 Tim 5:8). So he decided to give the £3,400 to his bride. When the day came for Charlie to make over this gift he met a response that echoed his own delight in giving. She too desired to wholly trust the Lord. God gave him a partner with the same call upon her life. Together they decided to give the last of their fortune into the hands of General Booth of the Salvation Army.

Here follow extracts from the letter they wrote together:

Dear General Booth,

I cannot tell you how many times the Lord has blessed me through reading your and Mrs Booth's addresses in the *War Cry*, and your books. And now we want to enclose a cheque for £1,500. The other £500 has gone to Commissioner Tucker (in India) for his wedding present. Besides this I'm instructing our bankers to sell our last earthly investment of £1,400 consols and send what they realise to you. Henceforth our bank is in heaven .... This step has been taken with reference to God's word and the command of the Lord Jesus who said, "Sell that ye may have and give alms. Make for yourselves purses which wax not old." And, "If you love me keep my commandments."

We thank God that now, as regards England, we are in the proud position of 'silver and gold have I none.' But we don't want to be like Ananias and Sapphira; we tell you honestly we have a small amount here .... Now there only remains one other command of the Lord Jesus for us to fulfil, "When thou doest thine alms let not thy left hand know what thy right hand doeth, that thine alms may be in secret." So we beg to sign ourselves . . . .My wife and me. NB. Please also enter the subscription as coming from "Go and do thou likewise."

We all know the story of the woman who came to Jesus with an alabaster jar of the most expensive perfume. She didn't give it to him to sell or to make money — she broke the jar and poured it over his head. Extravagantly it ran down all over her Lord. The fragrance filled the house and could never be gathered back into the jar. The shocked onlookers shouted, 'What are you doing? What a waste!' But the Lord said, 'She has done a beautiful thing for me. What she has done will be told in memory of her' (Mark 14:3-9). In reckless extravagance she poured all she had on the head of the one she loved.

Charles Studd poured out his money with the same motivation of heart. In reckless extravagance all was placed at the Master's feet. And the Lord was pleased with him.

Whatever financial difficulties he encountered in future years, we know God looks upon the heart. He received from Charles Studd an exuberant demonstration of his total trust, his utter abandonment to his Lord. Charles and his wife never turned back from their decision nor regretted it. Faithfully for the rest of their lives they delighted to live by faith, never making their needs known except to God. C T Studd lived as Hudson Taylor described, 'From God's hand to my mouth.'

CHAPTER TEN

AN ENCOUNTER OF
THE HEART

ONCE CHARLES STUDD was free to travel, he made for the coast to meet his brother George who was touring in warmer latitudes for the sake of his health and to avoid the British winter. Charles arrived in Shanghai in April 1887, two weeks before George, but soon found plenty to occupy his time. The Chinese he spoke was a different dialect to that of the coastal people, so he gave his attention to the crews of visiting ships.

The Mission to Sailors, near to the port, attracted many lonely young men. Each evening at the meetings many were saved. CT's eyes glinted at the opportunity of getting in among these men. Soon he was preaching, giving his testimony and leading men to Christ.

When George arrived, again in a somewhat backslidden state, he shared Charlie's bedroom, but had no intention of staying. He booked his passage to travel on to Japan the following week. Charles had grown in sensitivity to the Spirit and realised it would be a blunder to confront his brother immediately. He kept quiet but thought, 'This is nothing but a chronic case of the fear of man.'

George spent his time at the club and then played cricket,

which advertised his presence as he made a huge score. Of course Charlie went to watch. Soon questions were being asked. 'What on earth happened to your brother?' 'What! He became a missionary?'

Not many days passed before the same company of people were marvelling at George, who gave the boldest of testimonies at a public meeting and showed himself to be as 'mad' as his brother. He cancelled his sailing to Japan and eventually travelled inland with Charles. The two brothers now happily spent their time in the sailors' home, and the weeks slipped by into months.

At the mission, a young lady who had recently arrived in China with CIM attracted Studd's attention. She was unfit to travel into the interior because she had heart trouble. Charlie said, 'I had noticed that she moved very slowly; it seemed a real labour for her to get upstairs. I thought that such a person should not have come to China. There was little prospect that she could endure the hardships of life in the interior.' A little later he was to change his opinion of Miss Priscilla Livingstone Stewart.

Evidently the meetings with the sailors were not only blessing the men, but also Miss Stewart. The Spirit of God came among them and Priscilla was notably changed. Charles Studd wrote to his mother, when trying to describe her, 'She is very agile and runs up the stairs two at a time!' God had healed and strengthened her, but above all he had renewed the fire in her spirit. Before long she was teaching the meeting Salvation Army songs and giving her testimony. Her lively contribution in the meetings earned her great appreciation.

In cities like Shanghai, the expatriate community continued to cultivate a little England, with 'The Club', polite conversation at mah-jong circles, and drawing-room tea parties. One day Priscilla went to a tea party and there told her story of how she found Christ. The Spirit of God rested

Priscilla Livingstone Stewart shortly after her conversion

upon Priscilla and no doubt those women were stunned by the power and simplicity of what they heard. Before the day was out she was asked to go to another such drawing-room function, and then another and another! Women were being saved and challenged. The tea parties buzzed with a different kind of conversation.

When Priscilla left Shanghai to begin her long journey inland, C T said, 'I suppose all good things have to come to an end.' He too made arrangements to journey back to Shansi and Lungan where he kept the 'good things' alive by a vigorous correspondence.

Priscilla Livingstone Stewart was born 28th August, 1864, in Lisburn, Belfast, Northern Ireland. She came from a wealthy Irish Protestant family. When she arrived in China she was twenty-four years old, most attractive, with blue eyes and lovely reddish-golden hair. Her sparkling personality and uncomplicated, extrovert ways won the hearts of all who met her.

She had grown up in a religious atmosphere. Her family belonged to the Church of England, but it was not until two uncles were converted during the 1859 revival that religion became an uncomfortable family issue. One of her uncles was extremely active in the Lord's work, opening his home for meetings for his employees; very reminiscent of Edward Studd. Frequently he invited well-known evangelists of the day who would then be entertained by Priscilla's parents. A number of times these visitors took the opportunity to confront Priscilla with her need of Christ. She became adept at side-stepping their forthright questions and reaffirmed to herself that she did not want to become a Christian. She said to herself, 'No, I am not going to have my face as long as a fiddle for anybody.' As the months followed into years she consistently refused the Lord. She said that, 'At eighteen years old I was becoming a mocker and a scoffer.'

Priscilla tells her own story:

A turning point came in my life when I went to stay with a gracious lady who had endured many serious trials. To look at her one would never have dreamt that she had a care in the world. She was constantly serene and joyful. Her whole demeanour impressed me. Soon I was to learn the secret of her life; she would say, "I'm in such difficulties, would you mind kneeling down and praying with me?" Before I could say a word, the lady was on her knees praying.

One evening this lady's father came in and said, "I am to take the service at the Salvation Army tonight, will you come with me?" She said, "Father, I've been out to a meeting this afternoon, but my friend here will come." Talk about a dog in heaven! If I could howl I would have done so!... I had to sit on the platform with him and I shall never, never forget that night with hundreds of Salvation Army lassies all round me. Their stiff collars and studs creaked as they moved, they took their rattles and flapped them round my head! I was in a state, but I got away and nobody asked me about my soul.

When I arrived home my attention was drawn to a pamphlet, written by General Booth, describing a terrible vision he had had of a lot of people shipwrecked. You could see the people with their heads above the water and their hands stretching out, and some of them on the rocks. Someone was telling how Jesus would return suddenly, and then the same awful sudden fate was going to overtake the unsaved.

Although Priscilla's life revolved round parties, balls and worldly social occasions, somehow she could not forget what she had read. She publicly smoked cigarettes, even betting her friends that she could smoke six in one evening. And she did! Her lifestyle blatantly declared, 'I'm no Christian!'

Happy and tired, Priscilla arrived home early one morning from a ball. Soon she was asleep, but when she woke her mind was full of a vivid dream she had had.

I dreamt that I was with a number of young people at a tennis party. While we were playing, suddenly the Lord Jesus appeared

and singled me out and said, "Depart from me, for I never knew
you." I looked around for my companions saying, "Never mind.
We'll all go to hell together!" But they had all disappeared. I
was alone and then I had the most awful, terrifying vision of
hell. The next day I was haunted with the words "depart from
me, I never knew you" and if I took up a book they were there on
the printed page; I just could not get away from them.

Then one day at my aunt's house a party of young people were
telling their experiences, so I told them of the story I'd read of
the vision of General Booth. This led to our talking about
visions and dreams being sent of God. I said, "God has nothing
to do with dreams. I know perfectly well at school when I
studied too hard, my body slept and my brain went on working.
I know when I eat certain things and they disagree with me, I
dream. God has nothing to do with dreams!" And then I told
about the awful nightmare after that dance, and it was nothing
to do with God. My aunt turned to me and said, "What was
your nightmare?" I found myself telling it without realising,
and when I came to the part of how I was taken to hell, I looked
at her and thought: "Oh, now I'm in for a goody-goody talk,"
and I burst out laughing. I said, "That was nothing else but the
result of lobster and champagne." She said, "If anybody has had
a warning from God you have in that dream. Give your heart to
the Lord Jesus at once."

I have no recollection of rising but found myself at the other
end of the long room kneeling. I said, "I have never decided for
God, but I will tonight." Somebody spoke to me and said,
"What are you doing here? Three months ago you said you
would never go this way." I knew that person was the devil. He
came and kneeled beside me and I recognised him; I knew him as
a friend. I have heard ministers say, "People are never converted
through fear." But I was. I said, "I'm afraid of hell," and as I said
the words, the power of evil disappeared and the Lord laid hold
of me. Another voice said: "Child, what is it you want?" I said,
"I would give anything to get to God, but I cannot."

Priscilla saw her whole life pass before her. She saw those
who had attempted to witness to her and realised that on each

occasion it was Jesus reaching out to her but she had refused him.

My heart was as black as the worst sinner on earth; I was so convicted of unbelief, mocking and scoffing, that I might have been the most hell-deserving sinner that ever lived. As I waited upon my knees there came before my eyes the most wonderful vision of Calvary's cross and Jesus Christ nailed there; the cross was brought so close I might have touched his blessed feet. I saw the nails driven there by men, the crown of thorns pressed upon the brow, and the blood flowing down. I found myself exclaiming aloud: "Why was he there?" and there came back a voice, "He was wounded for our transgressions, he was bruised for our iniquities, by his stripes we are healed." It did not stop there, for he gave me a personal word: "With my stripes *you* are healed." The vision of the cross disappeared and I rose from my knees. I had been there two hours. My hostess said, "What have you seen?" I said, "I have seen Calvary, and for ever Jesus will be my Lord and my God."

Priscilla immediately went to her room and fell upon her knees and began to pray.

In her conversion Priscilla received the forgiveness of her sins and an incredible zeal to tell every person she met.

My own religious relations said, "Why, she was the blackest of the black sheep; if she is converted there is hope for anybody." I went to the Salvation Army and I said, "Colonel, I'm saved, I was saved last night." He said, "You were saved when you were at the meeting the other day surely." I said, "No, I was not and you never spoke to me."

She found the Salvation Army meetings a great joy. She walked in their processions.

I tell you it was worthwhile going with the Salvation Army; there were old boots, wood, stones, rotten eggs and oranges

86

thrown at us. They were grand days. None of my friends acknowledged me in the street, and the young men who were fond of me walked on the other side.

Within eighteen months this young firebrand was out training to be a missionary and before she was two years old in Christ she was on China's soil.

The stalwart Priscilla joined Miss J Burroughs and two other fearless soldiers of Christ, both unmarried ladies, living in Hoh-chau. These women showed incredible courage and were undaunted by the impossible opposition ranged against them.

How we longed to get the gospel message taken to every house in that great city. But no woman was allowed to walk in the street. If we wanted to go for an airing, an old, rickety, springless cart would be backed into our courtyard and a curtain drawn around. That was all the airing we got. If we went to see a woman our cart was backed into that woman's courtyard and we got out. No man was allowed to look upon any woman in that city, and yet it was none the better for it. It was the most wicked city.

When they looked at us they said, "You have the faces of women but you are men; you are men dressed up as women to decoy our womenfolk away." They were continuously curious about us and could hardly receive us as human beings. They said we painted our faces, but it was only the natural pinkness of our cheeks; then they said, "Look at her hair; it's the colour of a cow's." We didn't get many compliments.

We put our heads together and prayed, for we didn't know how to reach the people. It was decided that I should go out the next morning and buy some silk at a shop and my teacher go with me. I walked in a proper way some yards behind him, then went into the shop, delaying as long as I could haggling over the price. We knew perfectly well that a large crowd would gather; then our teacher could talk to them. We risked our reputation to go out and preach the gospel.

Pastor Hsi visited us and we told him what we were doing. He agreed to institute an open-air outside our own door. It was March, sleeting and snowing. The street was running with water and melted snow but we had on our padded cotton trousers. While he preached we four got on our knees and prayed. He went away having given us the courage to do the same ourselves. I never saw tears in a Chinaman's eyes excepting those days when we girls knelt and prayed for their souls.

Confronted by the thick darkness about them, Priscilla and Miss Burroughs were prompted to write home to share their concern. The people seemed to be literally possessed by the devil. They wrote, 'They are held in bondage, spellbound, deafened, blinded, hardened by the devil, indeed dead in trespasses and sins.' The two women were stirred to consider, 'Does the Bible teach us that there is a stronger power?' As God uprooted the unbelief in their own hearts, these dear women began to know with every fibre of their being that the Son of God came to destroy the works of the devil. Priscilla said,

How it makes one's heart rejoice and one's brain almost reel! He has sent us forth certain of victory. We are more than conquerors through him. What a glorious thought, "more than conquerors through him"! Nothing is impossible; we shall do exploits and be strong.

They entered into a covenant with the Lord to seek him with all their hearts for the salvation of souls. The Lord confronted them with the question, 'Am I risking anything for Jesus here in China or am I shielding myself from the reproach and shrinking from the cross?' Priscilla wrote, 'Our cry goes up to God, "Lord Jesus, if salvation means anything to me, let me live among these people as if I believed in eternity, and let me show them that I'm willing to risk anything—my very life if needs be—to rescue them from hell."' These women's hearts were broken before God as they saw the need all about them, but their efforts to preach the gospel were hindered by the conventions and traditions of Chinese culture and society. Regardless, they decided to take the gospel to where the people were.

> We went out to a large open space not far from the house, and had a meeting. The Lord manifestly set his seal upon it, praise the Lord. He brought the people in large numbers and as we stood there we felt as never before in our lives, the living God is among us. He laid hold of the people by the power of the Holy Spirit, There was no disturbance whatever—on the contrary, perfect quiet and attention; women joined us too, and the little children. We have been out three Sundays, and praise the Lord, he has given us victory from the very first. Some who had never ventured before, both men and women, have since come to our indoor worship. We believe that our going out and letting them see what our worship is like will win their confidence. Last Sunday forty women, some of the better class joined us, doubling the number of men. The Lion of Judah shall break every chain and give us the victory again and again.

Priscilla's first year in China passed, learning the language and being part of this daring pioneer work. The prolific correspondence with Charles Studd was the only interloper into her intense, concentrated life.

Probationary missionaries were required to remain unmarried for two years while they became accustomed to Chinese life and learnt the language. This did not hinder Charles from proposing marriage! Almost as soon as they had parted he contemplated Priscilla as his wife.

CHAPTER ELEVEN

FINDING
HIS OWN IDENTITY

WHEN STUDD ARRIVED back at Lungan with his brother, he was ready with a new vigour to get into the fight. He had enjoyed his days in Shanghai. It had been so good to be able to communicate and be fruitful again.

Studd had now spent two years in China. He had been slow to settle down and his protracted visit to Shanghai had prompted a few letters to fly about. 'C T S is not keeping in close touch; he is too independent. I shall be glad when he can have a helpful companion,' wrote Hudson Taylor. Studd continued as an associate missionary, and it seems his exposure to the mission did not encourage him to cast his lot in with them altogether.

His inclination to the Salvation Army and their methods was perhaps one of the reasons. The Salvation Army songs that Priscilla sang and the militancy of their gospel appealed to him. A letter received from Booth-Tucker, a Salvationist in India, had especially excited him. He longed to emulate their sacrifice and boldly demonstrate the gospel with street preaching, processions and bands. It appears that both Stanley Smith and Charles Studd did adopt their evangelising methods despite Hudson Taylor's disquiet. He wrote, 'There is a danger of our excitable brethren in Shansi going too fast.' It appears that Studd had appealed to the Salvation Army to come and help him in the work. Hudson Taylor goes on,

> A reckless Salvation Army band might easily drive us all out of any province in China... Every movement is reported by the mandarins to the provincial capital. They are apt to be alarmed. All the more reason for Studd to try his hand in Mongolia, perhaps with Cecil Polhill-Turner.

Abruptly all his plans came to a halt when Studd was smitten with typhoid fever, followed by pleurisy and pneumonia. He was extremely ill for some weeks. Fortunately his brother was able to nurse him till strength returned. His convalescence gave him time to further his avid correspondence with Priscilla. On one occasion he wrote two letters running into sixty-eight and sixty-nine pages respectively!

He proposed to her, but to his shocked amazement she refused him! Studd was never to be deterred. After a time of deep soul-searching, and eight days of fasting and prayer, he wrote again in the most confident fashion. Priscilla, many years later, said,

> If he were here he would tell you, I had proposed to him. I did not. As a matter of fact for certain reasons I refused him. And when I tell you his answer, you will see it is just characteristic of the man. He said, "You have neither the mind of God, nor the will of God in the matter, but I have. And I intend to marry you whether you will or not, so you'd better make up your mind and accept the situation." What was I to do? That is the reason why I'm Mrs C T today!

Month after month the debate continued by letter. He wrote on July 25th,

I only get more and more convinced about it, and I cannot doubt it is of the Lord, for you know how I've spent the time since receiving your letter: everything else has been laid aside, occupation, sleep and food, and I've sought his face to know his will. He has led me straight forward and day by day he speaks to me and gives me encouragement and emboldens me to ask definitely for you.

But it wasn't until October 5th that Priscilla gave her consent. Perhaps she held out for so long because she knew her engagement would mean resigning and becoming an associate with the CIM.

During these months when Studd so desperately wanted to know the mind of the Lord, his restlessness spilled over into all his relationships. This prompted Hudson Taylor to write in a fatherly way concerning him, 'I'm so glad you will meet him: without prayer and care I fear trouble might easily arise. Some of Studd's recent letters to friends suggest he is not happy, which makes them concerned.' Then in another letter a few weeks later Hudson Taylor goes on to say,

There are many indications which show that a good deal of care will be needed if we do not mean to drive him away. I am wondering whether it would be good for Studd and Cecil Polhill-Turner to go to Mongolia. I think you will, in that way, prevent their unsettledness from damaging others . . . both have felt some interest in Tibet. Pray about this and do what you think is right.

It appears that 1887 was a difficult year for Studd. He seemed to walk out of step with the mission, but his own personal relationships with individuals were excellent. He was greatly loved by those with whom he worked, and although separated, strong ties remained between him and the Cambridge Seven.

The year ended with Hudson Taylor saying, 'We must do

all we can to knit him more closely to us for *his own sake*. We can do better without him than he can without us.'

What was happening in C T Studd? Was he just a rebel? He certainly wasn't the kind of new missionary many would look for today. A rebel is one who wants to please himself, and throws off restraint for his own purposes. But C T Studd was entirely given to God and wholly available to do his will. His conversation and prayer revealed his heart. He was not a rebel. That issue was settled. His only desire was for the glory of Jesus. He wanted to see him magnified and desired above everything else to please and serve him. A deep principle of C T Studd's life was that he should be dead to himself, his own will and desires, so that God could have his perfect way. There was never a whiff of desire for self-glory or 'my work'. He had a sincere, transparent heart, and God who looks upon hearts knew Charles Studd was not a rebel.

Two years in China were time enough for Studd to begin to flex his pioneer muscles. His independence in thought, vision and action flowed from the pioneer blood in his veins. Such a person does not happily fit into the mould of other people's ideas. If asked to walk in another's footsteps, he will drag his feet. He is God's man to carve out the new way, then others will follow him.

The problems Studd encountered were because the pioneer spirit didn't produce instantaneous maturity. Hudson Taylor, the wise old owl looking on, must have had many a qualm, but perhaps he also had the wisdom to recognise that he was handling a future trail-blazer.

The courtship of Priscilla continued by letter. Charles poured out his heart on endless pages to his beloved. Every expression of his love was inseparably entwined with his consuming passion for his Lord. He wrote,

Now before I go further, I just want to beseech you, darling, that we both make the same request every day to our Father, that we may give each other up to Jesus every single day of our lives to be separated or not just as he pleases, that neither of us ever make an idol of the other.

He went on to say,

I laugh when I think of how little I know of you my own darling, not even your age or anything, only it's more than enough for me that you are a true child and lover of the Lord Jesus, that he has knit my heart to yours and yours to mine to work together for him with all our hearts and souls and minds till he come. . . . I love you for your love to Jesus, I love you for your zeal towards him, I love you for your faith in him, I love you for your love of souls, I love you for loving me, I love you for your own self, I love you for ever and for ever. I love you because Jesus has used you to bless me and fire my soul. I love you because you will always be a red-hot poker making me run faster. Lord Jesus how can I ever thank you enough for such a gift?

Time came for him to share his good news with his mother. He wrote,

I suppose you want to know about her. Well to tell you the truth I can't tell you much except about her spiritual life . . . she can play the harmonium or organ and sing a bit, but her voice wasn't wonderful in Shanghai. She's very fond of Salvation Army hymns, so am I, and the Salvation Army too, so am I, and she doesn't fear the face of man or woman a little bit, but just fires away at everybody she meets about their souls.

In jest some years earlier, C T Studd and other young bachelors were talking about marriage. At that time he said, 'Well, please God, I don't want to marry, but if I do, I want to marry a real Salvation Army lassie,' at which they all laughed. Well, it seems the Lord took Studd at his word and gave him his heart's desire.

No date was fixed for their wedding, but suddenly

arrangements happened in normal Studd impulsive fashion.

News arrived on December 26th, 1887, from Miss Burroughs, Priscilla's friend. Charlie read the letter to Stanley Smith; Priscilla had pneumonia. Though it was late the two men prayed—Stanley said, 'The most beautiful bit of resignation I've ever heard.' The letter had taken three days to arrive so without delay Charlie packed his few things and they negotiated for a cart which guaranteed to be there in three bone-shaking days.

No doubt they had a most fond meeting, their first since leaving Shanghai. Priscilla was much improved, the crisis was over and by the time Stanley Smith arrived a few days later, she was nearly well. Stanley said, 'I was deeply grateful for giving Miss Stewart to Charlie and, seeing her, she is indeed all Charlie says she is.' The two men were most impressed by the exceptional work these women were doing. Stanley said, 'In some ways it was the finest Chinese meeting I've been to in China.' On January 9th both men were to leave. After a time of praise in Priscilla's room they set off to Hungtung, arriving just before midnight. Unfortunately they were to go no further. On January 18th Stanley developed typhus fever and Charlie remained there until February 5th, nursing him day and night with much love and tenderness.

Priscilla was never far from Charlie's thoughts. When Stanley was fit Charles decided not to return to his station but to go back to Hoh-chau, to meet Priscilla. At Charles' appearance the local Christians said that if he had come so far to meet her, they should be married. Charles agreed!

To be officially married they needed to travel to an English consul; that meant the long journey to the coast. So that they could travel together respectably, they first had to have a Chinese wedding. Hurriedly arrangements were made. Pastor Hsi, a close friend and well-known itinerate evangelist, agreed to conduct the ceremony.

A wedding is an important, solemn occasion in almost any society and it demands recognition with new clothes. Pastor Hsi could not understand Charles' casual attitude and insisted he wore a new hat and a pair of shoes, which he produced. Unfortunately the shoes were so tight, Studd slipped them off during the ceremony. Priscilla graced the occasion with the addition of a long white sash with the words 'United to fight for Jesus' written across it.

At Tientsin they were married by the consul in their ordinary, native, calico clothes, to the shocked horror of friends. It was a simple matter of priorities: Studd could see no reason for spending money on wedding clothes. They would be legally married whatever they wore. He had the same attitude to a wedding ring. Priscilla had been presented with a simple gold ring by a very dear friend before leaving for China. By coincidence the letters CTS were engraved on the inside. Charles said, 'When it came to the day of our wedding, I said, "There's none like it and I'll not be married with any other."' It sufficed for eight years until Priscilla got home. Then Charles' dear mother said, 'Where is your wedding ring?' Charles' mother was not very impressed! Priscilla said, 'Charlie will never buy another.' Mrs Studd rummaged and found Charlie's grandmother's wedding ring and immediately put it on Priscilla's finger. Charles, in characteristic style, said, 'I never bought a ring. Peter's word about jewellery was quite good enough to stop any of that nonsense.'

It was May 16th, 1888. Early in the morning, a little after five o'clock, Charles arrived at Lungan with his new wife, now united to fight for Jesus and defeat the devil on his own ground.

CHAPTER TWELVE

IDENTIFICATION AND SUFFERING IN CHINA

LIFE NEVER STOOD still for the young couple as they returned to Lungan; immediately they were in the thick of the battle. Another house had to be acquired and the only one available was haunted; but no doubt the new praising occupants soon drove the devils out. Miss Burroughs, Priscilla's friend, joined them in the work.

The little foreign community lived in just the same manner as the people round about them, wore the same clothes and ate the same food. Their house was very basic with white-washed stone walls and uneven brick floors. The raised brick bed was heated and a thin, cotton-wool padded quilt, served as a mattress. In the centre of the room a Chinese-style clay boiler belched its fumes through a hole in the roof. This aggravated CT's chest. He was inclined to asthma. Eventually they replaced the monstrosity with something more efficient, to the amazed curiosity of their neighbours.

Millett was the local grain and when ground was served thick for breakfast, thinner for dinner, and thinner still for supper! In season, vegetables were available, and they learned to enjoy many Chinese specialities. They tried to make their own bread and produced something which approximated an English loaf.

Lungan was not an easy place to begin married life. It was a large city with about 10,000 Muslims living among a majority of spirit worshippers. Mr and Mrs Studd endeavoured to befriend their neighbours, who were eventually wooed into visiting their home. Visiting meant that unabashed meddlers did a thorough scrutiny of everything and every corner of the house. Like ants running everywhere, nothing was out of bounds. The people's curiosity did little to smother their blatant animosity to the 'foreign devils'; daily they received abuse and curses.

The mandarins, whose word was law, did not want them in the city, so no one else dared to befriend them. Priscilla said, 'For five years we never went out of the house without a volley of curses from our neighbours. Of course everything that happened in the city the Chinese blamed on us. There was a year of drought. Our lives were at stake, for they held us responsible.' It was deemed necessary to appease the rain god, so the Chinese went to bring one from another city. It was to be paraded so that the sun should fall upon its head. On a certain day placards went up saying that everybody was to have their big doors shut in their courtyards, and outside should burn incense to this rain god. Priscilla said, 'They knew we would not place incense outside our door, which would be considered a great insult to the god so that he would withold the rain. They meant to riot outside our house.'

The mob began to fire their house and pull down the chapel, so C T quickly turned all the Chinese out for their own safety and told them to go home. Priscilla was very ill at the time, so he carried her into the courtyard, climbed over the wall and ran to see the mandarins, but wisely they had left the city. Suddenly God intervened and came to their rescue. Among the crowd was an educated man, who could always command a certain amount of respect. He shouted, 'What are you doing? While you are wasting time, the day is passing. Pick up the god and go quickly so that the sun can come on his head. Take him and then come here on your way back.' The people meekly picked up the god and walked away to where the rich people lived. They looted their houses and stole silver to give to the city from which they had borrowed the god!

Chinese society of that period was incredibly cruel and ruled by fear. Life was of little value, especially that of baby girls. Priscilla wrote,

> Once I went into a mother's house and found her groaning, and I asked where the baby was. It had been born at daylight and immediately thrown into the moat. Sometimes they were thrown onto the mountainside or into pagodas built for this purpose, with a certain hole so that wolves can jump in and get the body when they want it.

How many times Priscilla went home broken-hearted.

Public executions were commonplace. Once Priscilla went into the square when highway robbers were to be beheaded. When asked, 'Why did you go?' she replied, 'To be strengthened for myself. I did not know when I might be going. I shall never forget how the man was dragged by a rope. Before he could reach the market square to be beheaded, he was lynched.'

Savage beatings were another form of punishment which many a Christian also endured. One of C T Studd's converts, a man who said, 'I'm a murderer, an adulterer and I've broken all the rules of God and man again and again,' was so gloriously converted that he felt compelled to go back to the town where he had done all his evil, 'To tell them of the good news.' Crowds gathered and he was brought before the mandarin and ordered 2,000 strokes with the bamboo until his back was raw, and he himself was thought to be dead. Some friends took him to the Christian hospital and nursed him till he was able to sit up. He then said, 'I must go back again.' Despite strong attempts to dissuade him, he went. Once more he was brought before the court. They were ashamed to give him the bamboo again, so they sent him to prison. There he preached the gospel through a tiny window to the crowd gathered outside, which caused such confusion they released him!

Despite opposition and many difficulties Charlie and his new wife endeavoured to preach the gospel. When interest seemed to wane they experimented by taking to the streets in a Salvation Army style procession, with C T Studd leading the way playing his banjo! Their sympathies with the Salvation Army grew, and it was even rumoured that they had joined the organisation. Some unauthorised declarations appeared in the Indian *War Cry* which caused a lot of concern in CIM circles. The phase passed after a few years when both Studd and Smith, who had also been involved, admitted that Salvation Army ostentation with drums and marching had not been successful. Hudson Taylor had made it quite plain he considered it the wrong method, especially as their presence in the region was barely tolerated.

The Studds were radical Christians. Courageously they challenged Chinese traditions where they cut across the ways of Christ. Custom decreed that Mrs Studd should walk behind her husband in the street. They walked together and ignored the mocking laughter. They did not intend being deliberately offensive but rather determined not to bow to customs and culture which were products of heathen attitudes. It was important to show that Christian marriage gives love and honour to the woman.

In old China abnormally tiny feet were considered correct for a woman, so from a young age they were required to have their feet bound to prevent natural growth. Consequently, the majority of women had grossly deformed and very painful feet. Strangely, custom decreed it taboo for a man to refer to a woman's feet, but Studd boldly waded in to explain the folly and cruelty of foot binding. He made a group of men imagine the pain and inconvenience of having a hand bound till it became useless and deformed, then he likened it to their wive's feet. The message was understood and the next candidates for baptism came with their feet loosed.

Their days were full of hardships, but as Priscilla and Charles observed the lives of the Chinese they had come to serve, they had no complaints. God allowed them to share their same kind of sufferings. Priscilla personally experienced the anguish the womenfolk endured in childbirth. When her first child was to be born, they had the alternative of travelling to medical help or remaining at home and managing by themselves. To go would mean leaving their work for a few months before the delivery and only returning when mother and baby were strong enough for the journey. The decision was soon made. They could not afford to be absent for so long; they would stay.

The sum total of their maternity knowledge was a two month course Priscilla had attended before leaving England. Charles had not had a similar advantage, though he possessed two medical books which gave a little information. When Priscilla went into labour she found herself having to be her own doctor, while her husband did his best as nurse. Studd said, 'I had an assistant. Our good friend Stanley Smith, in the adjoining room, was acting the part of an angel and never ceased to pray for us. Dr Jesus managed things perfectly!' A lovely baby girl was born. Fortunately a little later a nurse arrived, as suddenly Priscilla became seriously ill. Some anxious days followed, then the nurse said, 'Mr Studd I've tried every mortal thing that I can think of, but nothing seems to have any effect. Mrs Studd gets rapidly worse. I fear I ought to tell you that I can give you no hope for her recovery.'

Studd was such a fighter! As he stared death in the face he wasn't going to yield an inch to the devil. The nurse said to him, 'If by some miracle God does spare her life, you must take her home at once.' At those words, an immediate riposte came straight from his spirit, 'Go home again! God never sent us here to make us fools!' With that violent attitude against the power of darkness he prayed for his wife.

Totally cast upon God, he knew only one thing remained—he should anoint her with oil and pray. Emotionally and physically exhausted, he went to his dying wife and in simple faith obeyed Scripture. The following morning Priscilla was a new woman.

Utterly grateful, Charles knew God had responded to his act of faith. He said, 'This is the only way we will ever live in China.' We do not know the exact nature of the illness that afflicted Priscilla, but it is possible that the effort of labour had aggravated her weak heart. Each time she gave birth she experienced unusual difficulties.

Four other children were born in similar circumstances to this courageous couple, and not once did they have a doctor in attendance.

At the birth of their second child, Priscilla experienced a baptism into the grief of many a Chinese woman, when their newborn baby boy died. Completely alone they endured their private agony, but when Stanley Smith heard that Priscilla too, was desperately ill, he came. He arrived just in time to help Charles, who had gone to the city to buy a little pigskin box to bury the beautiful little body. Priscilla wrote,

I was left alone in my room. I shall never forget that experience. It has stuck with me throughout life. I felt absolutely broken-hearted. The question was whether I was going to give in and the whole of my missionary life be wrecked. Whilst Mr Studd was away I made a mark in my Bible. I made a covenant with my God that I was not going to let sorrow of any kind come into my life and ruin my life as a missionary. I was not going to let my husband see sorrow that would unhinge him. He never saw a tear when he came back.

On January 24th, 1890, Priscilla recorded the birth of Paul Snowball Studd in her Bible and added a little verse:

> Tis my happiness below,
> Not to live without the cross,
> But my Saviour's power to know,
> Sanctifying every loss.

Even in her weakness Priscilla summoned up strength to direct her will. She embraced the suffering and said, 'I will go on.' In God, this indomitable lady found resources to carry her through. Her behaviour must have spoken volumes to those who watched.

Her experience was common to womankind, but her reaction was totally different—she found grace in God. The hopeless grief of people without Christ tore Priscilla's heart. She said,

I shall never forget hearing a woman weeping for her child, her only child. A most extraordinary sound was coming over my courtyard wall, it was almost unreal, it haunted me. Someone translated and said, "It is your neighbour who has lost her child." It was the most awful noise I'd ever heard. Oh what a change when we know that we shall see our loved ones again!

After they returned to England, Priscilla had a son in Manchester, but he died after only four days.

In 1889 C T and his wife were still living at Lungan where they had purchased a good property for the work. They were both now listed as associates with CIM, but that did not hinder the mission sending Stanley Smith and his wife to join Charles at Lungan. The work was expanding, although progress was slow. The area seemed resistant to the gospel in comparison to other regions, possibly because of the Muslim influence.

Besides establishing a church, a refuge for opium addicts was opened. At first only a few hopeless men ventured to seek help, but when they left delivered, many more were encouraged to come. Pastor Hsi, the one who had married Priscilla and Charles, joined them in the work. His help was invaluable, but his fiery temper and powerful personality made it difficult for the highly animated Smith and Studd. Many a time their relationship came to ignition point.

Although men were the prime victims, the curse of opium addiction touched all levels of society, both men and women. Even little girls sought its anaesthetising power to dull the fear that swamped them as they contemplated their future. There was no joy anticipating marriage as a fourth or fifth bride to an old man. The only prospect was a life of drudgery, the slave of the other wives, to be beaten at whim for all or any failing.

During the seven years, about eight hundred men and women passed through the refuge, and some went away saved as well as cured.

Besides the refuge work they ran a dispensary. Every day suffering people would seek their help. With the aid of a couple of medical books and a big dose of common sense, they were able to assist most. Priscilla said, 'In seven years we never killed anybody!' Charles became quite an expert amateur doctor, boldly prescribing with one finger in a tome on pharmacology.

Studd's dabble with medicine gave him confidence for the rest of his life to do his own doctoring. When, some years later, he was admitted to hospital, he asked exhaustive questions and made copious notes on all treatments and medicines for future reference. He had an inbuilt reaction to the general caution of trained medical people; he wanted to make his own judgements and tried to gain enough knowledge to do so with some understanding.

By 1890 a new station was opened at Lucheng under the leadership of Stanley Smith and his wife. The Studds remained in Lungan doing an independent work. Their names were dropped from the list of CIM associates. Now, from choice, they were on their own.

Priscilla had come to China with a personal call upon her life. She had not followed a husband to the mission field and now, in marriage, she did not abdicate her courageous, willing obedience to the Lord. When it was necessary to go alone into situations she was not one to hold back. When people came from a long distance over the mountains asking for someone to go and preach the gospel in their city, it was decided that Priscilla should go in the care of one of the converts. She started out in a cart with no springs; the top part was loose from the wheels because the wheels were left behind while they crossed the mountain and travelled down the rocks. She said, 'I had to hold on for dear life. We arrived just about sundown, but one cannot stay outside the city after sundown because of robbers and wolves.' There appeared to be some disturbance in the city as crowds of people were coming out. Some Russians, who had been helping the people in a mineral mining enterprise, were being turned out and no-one else was being allowed in. 'Well,' said Priscilla, 'I've got to get in.'

> We pushed our way in and got to where I was to stay, and the gate inside the courtyard was closed. It is a great insult to close your gate in the city so the people shouted, "We will get in if you don't let us in." I went into the house to pray but they said, "Don't bring your God in here." So I went into the middle of the courtyard while all the people peeped out of their windows. We prayed and then I said to the elder, "Open the door." "I cannot. If I do not take care of you, what will Pastor Studd say?" I said, "We must have the door open," and when we did the whole

courtyard was full. They said, "Where is the foreign devil?" Like a flash it came to me and I said, "Where is the devil? I've never seen him. The devil is not here. I've come to bring you good news. Why do you curse me?" They came crowding round me and said, "You're absolutely different to us, look at your skin. Did they starve you? And why is your hair that colour?" It's considered that if a Chinaman has brown hair he must be suffering from malnutrition. They said, "We hear that you've got a hole through you for the pole of the rickshaw to go through." The women asked me very personal questions before the men, then they turned round and laughed. "She's only a woman, leave her alone." I stayed in the city for a whole week and we preached the gospel to them.

Charles said of Priscilla,

She spoke not from books, nor from the study, nor even from meditation; her speaking was from vision and from communion. What she believed, she saw and as she saw she spoke, and for that reason she had much effect upon her audience.

Financially they passed through many trials. Their money had been given away or ploughed into the work, but no immediate hundredfold return was theirs. Priscilla wrote to her family after her marriage telling them that her husband had given away all his money, and therefore would they continue to send the £50 a year as before. We do not know if that was their only regular support. For some period CT's family knew nothing of his circumstances; but whatever the extremity of his need, Studd had no intention of doing other than making his request known only to God.

It is no surprise, because it generally happens to those who walk this way of faith, that there came a time when the last of their supplies were finished and there was no apparent hope of relief. The mail only came once a fortnight, so if the postman brought nothing they would starve. They put the children to bed and agreed to pray through the night about their predicament. But after only twenty minutes they rose from their knees. They had told God everything. There seemed no point in carrying on as if he were deaf or could not understand the desperate situation.

The mail man returned at his appointed time. Hurriedly they glanced over the letters; there was nothing. Their eyes met. Charles took the mail bag by the corners and shook it. Out fell a letter in unfamiliar handwriting. Ripping it open, Charles read, 'I have for some reason or another received a command of God to send you a cheque of £100. I've never met you, I've only heard of you, and that not often, but God's prevented me from sleeping tonight by his command. Why he should command me to send you this I do not know—you will know better than I. Anyhow here it is and I hope it will do you good.' The signature meant nothing to either of them; with awesome thankfulness they praised the Lord.

*   *   *

Increasingly asthma became a major problem to Studd and hindered his normal life. He had been in China for eight years and physically it had taken its toll on them both. In May 1893, news of Charles' poor health reached his mother. Her immediate response was to send him money for the whole family to return home, but over a year passed before they eventually made the long journey.

Hudson Taylor met the Studds at Shunteh before they left China. He reported on that meeting,

I was glad to find C T much better. As soon as he got on lower ground his breathing improved. Though very weak on starting and unable to walk any distance, the last day he walked eighteen miles. I found him and his wife in a beautiful spirit, and their children looking well. He has given over his large premises to the work of the CIM. I wished to take charge of it *for him*, not to accept it as an unconditional gift, but he much preferred the latter, as it would leave us free to develop it as we desire and are able. So I accepted it. When I got to Lungan, I was much pleased with the work. The premises are larger than I should have chosen, but on the other hand could be adapted for a large central work.

With the work and the property in good hands Studd left China, sick in body but rejoicing in spirit, fully intending to return when his health had recovered.

Japan was at war with China and any movement of 'foreign devils' caused much consternation. Their lives were constantly in danger. Two young Christian men escorted them to the coast. Travelling with four small children was not an easy task. When they reached Shanghai it dawned upon these two that the time for separation had come. In front of the whole ship's company these Chinese men stood sobbing. Everybody heard them. As Studd waved his last farewell, a fellow passenger touched his arm and said, 'Well Mr Studd, you didn't come out to China for nothing.'

CHAPTER THIRTEEN

MINISTRY IN THE UNITED STATES

T HE STUDDS RETURNED to England in 1894. Charles' ever-loving mother opened her heart and her home. All were welcomed—Priscilla whom she had never met, and their four boisterous girls. Every provision was made, with rooms on the third floor of Hyde Park Gardens and a nurse for the children. For a time it was wonderful to relax and enjoy the bounty that was showered upon them. Charles didn't take too kindly to being fitted out with 'proper' clothes, but the girls delighted in fussy silk dresses, bouncy petticoats, ringlets and ribbons. Travelling in granny's carriage was somewhat more comfortable than the Chinese cart!

A little rest and recuperation soon saw the whole family looking fitter. Grandmother was well-known for the exceptional spread at her dinner table. No doubt this contributed to Priscilla and Charlie regaining their health.

Charlie had a thorough medical check, most probably at his mother's insistence, where it was confirmed that though he had asthma there was not permanent lung disease. Priscilla's problem was more grave. She had an incurable heart condition which was alleviated by the easier lifestyle she enjoyed in London.

Once Charles was rested and his strength regained he was ready for work. Opportunities for ministry opened in many towns and cities of the British Isles. With the family settled at Hyde Park Gardens, nothing need stop him.

Graciously the Lord provided for him and the family. Certain wealthy friends regularly gave gifts, but they were never sufficient to make him financially free from his family, who continued to support him. It was a suffering he had to bear for many years. He couldn't choose the way in which God would supply all his needs.

It was not surprising that when news reached the United States that Charles had returned from China, an invitation was received for him to come for a tour of the universities. After the Cambridge Seven had sailed, Charlie's brother Kynaston had toured in the States telling their story and encouraging others to follow their example. The Student Volunteer Movement grew out of this, and its founder, John Mott, was led to Christ by Kynaston during that tour.

Studd arrived in America in 1896 to a pre-planned, hectic itinerary. He travelled from university to university, spending from a few days to weeks in each. November saw him moving every day or two whilst taking at least one meeting and sometimes as many as five in one day. Between meetings he had appointments with individuals. He led many to the Lord, and counselled dozens of others through to total consecration of their lives and the fullness of the Holy Spirit. December saw him travelling from Nebraska to Kentucky with many stops in between: January, Columbia to Pennsylvania; February, Ohio; March, Indiana to Kentucky; and so we could go on. He visited all kinds of colleges and ministered to all kinds of students.

Spiritually, nothing could satisfy Studd more. He said, 'This life is just lovely. Everywhere souls are lighting up. God has prepared them.' The evangelist Studd overflowed with satisfaction. Again and again he would be invited to speak in the local churches. God opened endless doors to him, and everywhere he went the Lord was blessing. Then at one conference he felt nothing was getting through. He didn't enjoy the preaching and wondered if it was his fault. He seemed to be hitting a brick wall. Afterwards many came and said what a powerful blessing the word was in their lives. There was much fruit and many further invitations flowed from that meeting. He said, 'I mustn't rely on my feelings or measure the result by my enjoyment.'

Charles wrote home every few days. His letters are like a diary of his travels, feelings, the ministry and the results. He was having a glorious time. When at Knox College he wrote, 'We had such freedom in prayer, we laughed, thanked and prayed. We were drunk in the Spirit.'

Charles was a very gifted personal worker. His straight-forward approach to spiritual problems rudely wrenched people out of the ethereal, into reality, to be faced with honesty and dealt with by a deliberate act of the will.

Backsliders squirmed as they saw their sin and understood how they were robbing God. The unconverted were left in no doubt about their position, but he was incredibly patient with those who meant business with God. He thought nothing of giving three hours of his 'spare time,' even if it were well into the early hours of the morning. Studd was a lover of men, a dynamic servant of God who rarely complained about the demands put upon him.

His aim, whether speaking to one or to thousands, was to see each person wholly consecrated to God, where no part of life was reserved for self, for personal desires and one's own way. His only satisfaction was to see men fully surrendered so that God could fully do his will.

As young men were brought to this glorious place of usefulness to God, Studd sought to seal their commitment with prayer, and then led them to receive the fullness of the Holy Spirit. He taught plainly that man's best intentions will come to nothing except he be empowered by the Holy Spirit. Carefully he led those resistant to the teaching to examine the lives of the disciples before and after Pentecost. The simplicity of his manner of instruction led hundreds into the place of power.

He said, 'The Lord's presence is so manifest, we are utterly surrendering ourselves and coming away so full, full of love, praising and rejoicing. Holiness is the wonderful by-product; glory, glory, hallelujah!'

Despite his gruelling schedule, he lived a disciplined life. His early morning prayer times were more than just important to him, they were the source of his life and strength. Out of his quiet times flowed a vital relationship with his God and lover. He delighted in the 'fairest of ten thousands'. The Song of Songs was his shared love letter; love to be received and love to overflow.

At home Priscilla was having a very difficult time. She was battling with her loneliness, the pettiness of the life she now lived and the weariness of family disapproval. She was alone to bring up the girls, and always the spectre of financial insecurity haunted her—and it seems the family didn't let her forget it.

Priscilla repeatedly asked Charlie if she could come to the States, but each time he refused her request. Among other factors, it seems the basis on which Charlie went precluded his wife. Charles' lifestyle left no place for a wife. He was convinced that her presence would have hindered the work because he would be less free to see the endless stream of young men who wished to talk to him. 'They would be shy,' he said, 'and you would be mainly alone whilst I travel.'

So often the hospitality he received from the students left much to be desired. Sometimes he arrived at a town and no one met him, or they forgot he too had to eat. Frequently there was no room provided, and very often he had to share a bed with one of the students! 'It's vile,' he said. Charles was right; it was no place for Priscilla.

Charles was always very honest. He occasionally had a grumble about the conditions—then he added, 'Don't tell anyone, I only growl at you. Pray!' The next morning he wrote, 'What a dreadful growl, I'm most ashamed of myself.'

He did all he could by his lengthy, frequent letters to encourage Priscilla. He recognised hers to be the hardest part. He was greatly concerned that she should remain the main influence upon the children, to bring them up to love God. Constantly he exhorted her to be a witness and carefully instructed her on how to receive the Holy Spirit, to give thanks, obey and rejoice.

In every letter he encouraged Priscilla to be on fire just like she was in Shanghai. The letters he received from home must have torn his heart many a time. Priscilla was frequently ill, and at times very ill. Charles had to face the fact that her health meant 'goodbye to China'.

One of her main provocations was living at Hyde Park Gardens. She found herself at loggerheads with the children's nurse, and the only solution she could envisage meant joining Charles in the States. The dilemma continued for months, making Priscilla frustrated and anxious. Their limited finances always prevented them from making their own arrangements. Priscilla even viewed a cottage for their own use, but it was beyond their means.

These pressures weighed heavily upon Charles. He said, 'The devil came along tonight and said, "You did play the fool in giving all away."' In a flash Charles returned a sword thrust of the word of God and put the devil to flight. He never dwelt upon doubts, and neither did Priscilla, even though they passed through many a trial hatched in hell to make them doubt and question. Charles said, 'The devil does tease and persecute. At times a dark shadow oppresses me.'

Studd's absence from home eased into a year and then eighteen months. The hardship began to have its toll in both of their lives. When Priscilla was sick again, Charles asked her, 'Is it my fault? Perhaps there has been something wrong with my life. Pray, ask God to show me.' His letters to Priscilla at this time were full of tenderness and loving instruction, looking for her best and helping her to keep a good attitude to his family.

At this period of his ministry he was so willing to admit his faults, a genuine humility shines through so much of what he wrote. At one college he confessed, 'I've taken a dislike for a man and I can't shake it off. Pray for me. I'm praying for him till my heart should be kept in love for him.' Sadly, this teachable attitude left him in his later years, a warning to us all. Constantly he was amazed at the goodness of God. He said, 'Ten meetings in two days. I'm dead tired; God is doing it in spite of me.'

His final few months were spent in much conflict. He saw such amazing results from his ministry, but glaring faults in himself. He was frequently ill. Asthma stalked him at every turn. Rarely did he get free, and for weeks he battled with chest infections and other illnesses which eventually carried him off to hospital.

He became depressed and talked gloomy talk. 'It seems I'm blacker far than the devil himself—I do hate myself more and more. I feel a perfect hypocrite and I wonder how God can let me go on like this.' The devil took his opportunity; he found Studd low and gave him a good kicking. But the warrior wouldn't lie down under that for long. Sitting up in bed wheezing, unable to sleep, he memorised chapter one of Philippians and rejoiced.

When the times were hard he buried himself deeper in the Lord. He said, 'I skipped breakfast and dinner to have more time with the Lord in prayer.'

Any marriage put through such stresses was likely to come under strain, and theirs was no exception. Trying to take a positive stance towards their continued separation, Studd says, 'It's God's goodness to us so that we learn to know him in deeper intimacy.' He exhorts Priscilla, 'Forget me now and concentrate upon Jesus; know him as your husband.' Sometimes her letters were not so frequent or as loving as he desired but, even then, he found in himself a positive attitude. He was sure that in the end their separation would cause them to love one another the more and make Priscilla long for him. He had a sneaking suspicion that she used to despise him a little.

Musing on marriage while feeling very ill, in a college room, with his washing hanging up over his head and eating his lunch off his lap, Charles said, 'We have to be careful that we do not make Jesus and his work pay too heavy a price for the demands of our marriage.' A sentiment that would be completely reversed in most Christians today.

After a short period in England he visited the United States again, but this time Priscilla accompanied him. Studd had an amazing admiration for his wife. He said,

She possessed an extraordinary personality. Wherever she went everybody seemed to confide in her. We travelled by ship and she was quite as good as a newspaper to me. She was always very careful about my health, so when Sunday came she would not let me speak more than once. The people insisted there should be a second meeting, so she took it and not a few were visibly affected as she spoke on our work in China. It became the talk of the ship. When we were returning to England, there happened to be one man on board who'd been on the same ship as we were coming out. In no time he told of that meeting on China, with the result that a deputation came to beg her to speak again. Nearly all the people turned up, and the effect was precisely the same.

Priscilla came to life whenever she had the opportunity for ministry.

Two people like Priscilla and Charles Studd could barely find spiritual satisfaction in the normal kind of ministry of the church in England. They were gifted as pioneer evangelists and doomed to continual frustration in traditional Christianised Britain. While their feet remained on home soil, their hearts were in the mission fields of the world. Within a short space of time the Lord began to open another door. He knew the desires of their hearts, so he led them to a place of surprising satisfaction.

CHAPTER FOURTEEN

INDIAN DELIGHT

I N THE BACK OF CHARLES' MIND lurked the idea that one day he should visit India. How he would love the opportunity to preach the gospel to the estate workers on his family's plantations! The thought excited him. His brother George had been there, and his report only quickened CT's interest so that he questioned: had the time come when God would open up the way?

Mr Vincent, his father's old friend, confirmed the Lord's will by offering to finance a visit. Studd was overjoyed. I wonder, as these events unfurled, if Priscilla's thoughts turned back to the time when she first committed her life to Christ? One day as she had sought guidance for her future, she saw in the margin of her open Bible the words: China, India, Africa. India was happening; would Africa follow?

Charles set sail once again on his own; this time heading for Tirhoot, North India. We know little of this phase in Studd's life, but no doubt, in his own inimitable way, he endeavoured to preach the gospel. His ardent desire to reach the Indian labourer would have been frustrated by the barrier of language, but that didn't hinder him from trying. The episode presented a big challenge in a culture he did not understand.

He found his best opportunity among relatives, his father's brothers and sisters. Some were business partners, others the children of his father's first marriage. He took his opportunity with the families of his half-brothers and sisters. He spent six months among them, and while there he received an interesting invitation to pastor a church in South India.

During his stay in Tirhoot, he came in contact with the work of the Anglo-Indian Evangelisation Society whose aim was to carry the gospel to the British expatriates isolated from Christian fellowship or witness. It was through this particular organisation that Studd learned about the Union Church in Ootacamund, a hill station with many resident British. The church had an evangelical reputation, a place of influence where notable preachers came.

Taking a ship from Calcutta, where he had grasped the opportunity to visit other family friends, he sailed to Madras and arrived in Ootacamund for Sunday, May 20th, 1900.

His coming caused no small stir. Mr T Staines, a notable local figure, wrote encouraging the church 'to give Mr Studd a hearty welcome.'

The agreement provided for Studd to give two-thirds of his time to the church, and with the remainder, to travel, visit and evangelise among the scattered Europeans. A good house, Elk Hill Lodge, was made available for him. He must have been overjoyed. He wrote to Priscilla thanking and praising the Lord that some of their hopes and dreams were coming true. They had both longed for a cottage by themselves. On one occasion Studd had written to Priscilla saying, 'And it would be better if it were abroad where the family can't see how we live and bring up the girls!'

As soon as possible, Priscilla made plans to join him. When he had been in the United States ministering to the students, she had commented that, 'They should pay you a regular salary.' Now for the first time in their married life, they were to receive one. Between the church and the society a salary was agreed. Priscilla expressed her satisfaction: a small prop of security. Charles was quick to re-emphasise to her that their trust was in God and not the salary. He said, 'If they pay our expenses, well and good, but I am not going to trust in God *and* them, I shall trust only in God and so will you.'

Priscilla arrived in Ootacamund in October 1900, and a new, more peaceful phase of life began to unfold for the family. What a joy for her to have her own home; she could now indulge herself in the pleasure of entertaining. Priscilla excelled in hospitality, and her position as the pastor's wife in a busy church afforded her plenty of opportunity.

Their daughters, aged from six to twelve years, revelled in the freedom of their new life. Their father, now frequently at home, could be such fun. He would take them out in the buggy, but instead of keeping to the main road he would attempt daring shortcuts up very steep paths where they all hung on for dear life. Visitors flowed in and out of the house. Young army officers with little to do happily played with the girls and escorted them on picnics and outings; then as they grew older, to parties and social events. Ootacamund was a very social place. The girls loved it. Long, happy days followed.

Ootacamund, 7,500 feet above sea level, provided a haven for the British in India. The climate, often wet and cool— almost too much like England—offered a welcome relief from the heat of the plains. It became increasingly popular as many army personnel were stationed there and brought their families. The hillsides were dotted with the well-appointed homes of army officers, retired government officials and successful businessmen. The club, with its rules, perpetuated a slice of British upper-class living in an alien land. Sport figured prominently; the British residents in Ootacamund could go riding, play polo, tennis, cricket, or golf on beautifully maintained, challenging courses, or go hunting and shooting. Life offered every luxury at a reasonable price, and the possibility of servants far in excess of one's wildest dreams in England of that day.

The roads had been improved and most had a hard surface, though cobbled. Transportation was still by bullock carts or horse-drawn carriages. Motor vehicles were the amazing exception. A rack railway had been constructed as far as Coonoor, eleven miles south and 2,000 feet below Ootacamund. Despite the difficulties a traveller encountered in reaching Ootacamund, its popularity only increased.

Ooty, as it is generally called, was the summer residence of the governor of Madras State. When he arrived 'the season' began. One certainly wonders how Charles and Priscilla, with their ideals, fitted into this scene. Studd appears to have made himself quickly at home, and on many an occasion was invited to Government House where he sat drinking tea from the finest bone china, whilst conversing with Lord and Lady Ampthill, the governor and his wife. Studd's immediate acceptance with the Governor General was guaranteed; they were both old Etonians. The Viceroy of India, Lord Curzon, and the Bishop of Madras, dignitaries of state and church all found their way to Ooty where C T was privileged to meet them.

The sophisticated foreign ways of the European ran parallel to the average Indian's life. Their paths rarely touched, except at the master-servant level. Language, culture, education, tradition and aspirations created mountains in between. Few crossed those barriers.

While the expatriate enjoyed his modified western life as best he could, Indian women trudged up the steep hills with impossible loads of firewood on their heads, boys idled behind the grazing animals as they trespassed, groups of men squatted round fires to keep warm, and barefooted families, like mountain goats, wended their way up steep grassy paths to their cold houses.

Poverty stalked the people; illness or capricious weather conditions could change a family's fortunes, so that those who had previously eaten well were virtually brought to begging. Life was hard.

CT's mission was not to these local people. Ootacamund Union Church had been built by Europeans for Europeans. The ministry was in English. It competed in the same small town with two other European churches, both Anglican, where those of the establishment automatically attended. There existed no guaranteed large pool from which the Union Church could draw its congregation. The 'Tin Church' as it was affectionately called was an amalgamation of non-conformists. Its influence and reputation had been established by the quality of the Bible teachers who served it.

Studd barely fitted the mould of pastor for such a congregation. First of all, he was an evangelist, and secondly he had little time for keeping Christians happy to attend church for the rest of their lives. He would not bring them a confortable word to make them feel good, or a sound teaching to add to their knowledge of the word of God—something more to not obey! He could only be himself—a forthright, zealous evangelist. He used every opportunity to fearlessly proclaim Christ in circles where such blatant witness was scorned. It was said of the church during Studd's time, 'I shouldn't go there unless you want to be converted!'

His amazing love of men drew him naturally to visit the regiments stationed in the locality. Among them he found a fruitful field—many soldiers owed their salvation to his faithful preaching. A number of officers became his close friends. He was welcomed by high-ranking men and their wives, who opened their homes to him and their lives to Christ.

Team sport figured high among the soldier's activities, so it was not long before Studd was regaining old form on the cricket field. He delighted them with two double centuries, and even toured with one regimental team. Every such event presented a unique chance to live with the men and be a witness.

Studd remained in India till 1906. Although the kind of ministry and way of life was hardly what we would have thought best suited him, it gave Priscilla and the girls a very welcome respite from family pressures. Ooty proved to be a delightful place for his daughters to grow up—where they were privileged to enjoy the pastimes of the rich without the income.

School continued at home with governesses sent out from England. The girls went through three during the six years at Ooty, in an effort to acquire the kind of education needed to equip them as young ladies. They didn't even miss out on music lessons and piano practice. God faithfully provided in his own way so that these girls received the kind of education that matched family expectation. In the future they took their place comfortably in family, society and the work of the

Pauline, Edith, Dorothy, and Grace when they went to India

Lord. The local ministry kept Charles at home for a good part of each month; just what his daughters needed. These were fun years, when the family grew together and the girls grew up.

Each child learned how to ride—the hard way, on a horse that threw them. Charles thought, 'It will teach them courage'! Early in the morning they would ride out two by two, with their father upon his much-loved, large Australian mount. He hadn't a son, so he attempted to squeeze his daughters into the role. Even when it came to cricket he could see no reason why they shouldn't learn the art. Out on the pitch Edith especially excelled; she was more inclined to be her father's 'boy'.

Ooty is a very poor place for an asthmatic. The altitude alone could prompt an attack, but more than that, there is hardly a level road in the district. Even a short walk entailed steep gradients which soon set Studd wheezing and panting. Life on the plains would have been easier for him in that respect. As he managed to play cricket there must have been times when he was fit, but in the winter months the climate, very wet and cold, is certainly unsuited to those with a weak chest. Priscilla said, when they were leaving India, 'Almost the slightest movement brings on another attack.'

As the time approached for them to return to England, Charles became concerned that his daughters should be baptised; their ages ranged between twelve and eighteen years. Some years earlier Charles had battled out the problem of infant baptism. He left the Anglican Church, much to the consternation of his family, and had refused to have his own children baptised as babies. Now he went ahead to prepare for them to be baptised as believers by immersion. Then followed a most unconventional baptismal service.

Quite an auspicious group gathered: missionaries, including Amy Carmichael, friends, church leaders, and the Anglican vicar. Each young person was quizzed concerning her personal faith by anyone present. They all passed the ordeal like experts. These girls knew what it was to belong to Jesus and could with all sincerity be baptised as believers. It must have been a very special joy for Priscilla and Charlie to see their own ones seal their salvation by public testimony.

The church had no baptismal pool, so Studd set out to construct one for the occasion. The gardener dug up the biggest flower-bed and made a large hole. Then a good-sized tank was brought from the bazaar and sunk into the ground. Relays of servants ran with warm water to fill it up, but soon they discovered they were racing against time. The tank had a leak! Studd, standing in another hole alongside the tank, immersed the girls one by one, and then they returned to the drawing room where they celebrated the breaking of bread in a most informal fashion.

Priscilla, Charles and the four young ladies were soon back at their grandmother's home in Hyde Park Gardens. Before the family could bombard Charlie with questions, such as, 'Now what is going to happen to your girls?' the Lord graciously intervened.

The three eldest were waved goodbye and sent to school in Switzerland. Eighteen months later they were speaking poor French. If Charles had still had his fortune, he would have chosen to send his daughters to Sherbourne School, considered the best girl's school in the country. Almost as if the Lord read his thoughts, the following term God provided for them and all but the youngest left for Sherbourne School.

Grace the eldest, was soon to be married. Childhood had flown and with it the opportunity to mould lives and shower them with love. Edith said, 'We knew mother loved us, but she seldom showed us any outward affection.' It seems that neither Charlie nor Priscilla were demonstrative in their love. The girls enjoyed their grandmother, the most approachable and loving person, to whom they could turn on any occasion.

Charlie again began an itinerate preaching ministry,

travelling all over the British Isles. Even though he was now forty-six years old, he could not feel settled in Britain. The complacent British church filled him with gloom. The mission field remained his concern, and before long his concern became a call. In 1908 God called C T Studd to his greatest task which would engage him till his dying day.

CHAPTER FIFTEEN

FIFTY NOT OUT!

I T'S BEEN SAID, 'Life begins at forty,' but what happens at fifty? For the pioneer it's a time of dilemma. Outwardly he sees his body growing older, but inwardly the deep motivations that have made him what he is are still urging him on. Dare-devil plans occupy his thoughts; hopes and visions fill the screen of his mind; passions surge in his soul. 'Why not have one more go?' he says. 'I'd rather go out in a blaze of fire than carefully fade like a finished wick.'

In 1908 when C T neared this dangerous age, 'by chance' he happened to be visiting Liverpool when he saw an intriguing notice: 'Cannibals want Missionaries'. CT's mind was the perfect, fruitful ground for such provocative advertising. To him, nothing sounded more inviting: cannibals— a chance to get to grips with a real challenge, to take the gospel into the stronghold of the devil! A sense of adventure is part of a pioneer's makeup, and this sounded like the ultimate enterprise.

The poster advertised meetings being held by a German missionary, Dr Karl Kumm. The intrepid man, it was said, had made a journey on foot right across Central Africa. He had observed first-hand how the Muslims were spreading south, sweeping upon whole populations who would be doubly lost to the cause of Christ once under the power of Islam. Passionately he presented the need of numberless tribes who had never heard of Christ. Urgently he called for support—missionaries were needed to open up stations to stem the onward march of the Muslims pushing down southwards into the vast continent.

The hidden interior of Africa was opening up. Already the trail was worn by traders and game hunters who lived off their kill. For centuries Arabs had plagued the continent in pursuit of the iniquitous slave trade; but now a host of modern curio-hunters, explorers and scientists were walking the ancient paths of the African. White faces were no longer unfamiliar; colonisation had brought European officials—but where were the missionaries? No one had gone to tell of Christ. C T Studd felt a personal shame. 'Oh God! How the church has failed!'

Dr Kumm was just the sort of man to whom C T Studd would relate—fearless and bold, one who had counted all things as loss to gain Christ. As the old German spoke, the Spirit of God did his own persuasive work: some parted with their money, others went away with a burden to pray, but C T found himself arrested by God. Was it purely chance that he happened to be there?

From the depths of his soul he cried out, 'God why have no Christians answered the call?' and the reply came, 'Why don't you go?' His first thought was, 'But it's too late, I'm sick, the doctors wouldn't permit it,' and immediately back came the answer, 'I am the God that heals you. Can't you trust me? I will go with you and keep you.'

The issue of obedience to God's will had been settled many years before. For C T Studd, to hear was to obey. God had spoken; he knew all he had to do was to follow. Complex emotions raced through his mind. What a thrill to go into the heart of Africa! What joy to take the gospel to those who had never heard the name of Jesus! As he contemplated the work he knew nothing would satisfy him more.

Stark reality had to be faced—he had no money, and how could he go at fifty years old, with his wife in poor health and only one of his four daughters married? Lurking in the back of his mind, although he didn't wish to admit it, was the painful knowledge that he himself would fail any medical examination.

Then brushing aside all the problems as if they were of no consequence, C T Studd was raring to go. Kumm and Studd decided to travel together, crossing Africa from east to west. Studd, fired in his spirit, wanted to plant the first in a string of mission stations right in the heart of Africa.

When he arrived home to his family, full of confidence with a new call upon his life, he met some of his stiffest opposition. His dear mother who for years had taken a loving, caring interest in Charlie's family was filled with horror. She openly wept and pleaded with him not to go— and Priscilla, his faithful wife, sobbed in her room on the third floor of Hyde Park Gardens. C T would not be moved by her pleading, as she cried out, 'Oh Charlie! How could you?'

The opinion of his four daughters would have had little effect upon him. His relationship with his children had always been somewhat remote, 'Father was so tough on the children,' commented Edith some years later.

With his eyes constantly fixed on the mission fields of the world he seemed to overlook his own flesh and blood. From his perspective he had no choice; he could hardly permit himself the legitimate luxury of family feelings. Although, to be perfectly fair to the enigmatic Studd, he wrote letters to each daughter, carefully and lovingly instructing them at crucial times in their lives.

The time drew near to sail, but at this point, C T had to admit, God intervened. As the ship pulled out of the harbour

C T was at home in bed with high fever—another attack of malaria. If he had sailed he would have done so against the advice of doctors and to the great hurt of his wife and family. God said, 'No.'

Despite the impulsive false start to take the gospel into the heart of Africa, C T didn't waver in his purpose. As soon as health and strength returned he tirelessly devoted himself to obeying the call of God. A new plan of action was drawn up, demonstrating yet again the wisdom of God. Studd, an independent 'out front' man, number one in any group of people, would have found difficulty being number two to Dr Kumm. That wasn't God's plan. He had other purposes for Studd.

In 1910 a World Missionary Conference was held in Edinburgh, Scotland, and C T Studd was there. The report by Mr John Mott, General Secretary of the World's Student Christian Federation, titled 'Carrying the Gospel to all the Non-Christian World', so fired C T Studd that he couldn't let the matter rest. His own personal copy of the report is closely marked. The extent of the need detailed in its pages cried out for response. Millions of unevangelised people were waiting for the gospel. Studd's childlike immediate reply was 'I'll go, I'll go.' As always, he was one to obey first and work out the problems later. His attempt to travel with Dr Kumm the previous year had failed, but the fire in his heart hadn't subsided. When Kumm took the platform at the convention, his powerful words fanned the flame of devotion in Studd's heart.

He listed twenty-six separate tribes not yet evangelised by Protestant missions, numbering from five thousand to two million, each along the borderline of Central Africa, marking the extent of Islamic infiltration. Dr Kumm challenged the conference, 'These tribes stand in the way of the advance of Islam.' Carefully he described their vulnerability, and Studd, like a wise army general, took in the seriousness of the need.

Dr Kumm completed his address with, 'These tribes living in the mountains of Central Sudan are the most warlike in Africa. They are worth winning, and it would be an eternal shame on our generation if we let those tribes go over to Islam.' Those words are marked in C T Studd's personal copy of that address. He was determined that by any means he would assist in removing that shame.

Two years elapsed between the time when C T first received the call to Africa to his eventual departure for an exploratory visit—two years during which his call became insistent and his family grew accustomed to his decision. At the same time, a base of prayer and financial concern was formed for his project. Waiting time in God's purposes is not wasted time.

C T was not getting younger or fitter. His physical condition presented a formidable obstacle which had to be overcome or ignored if he were to fulfil his heart's desire. He still suffered with asthma and recurring bouts of fever. Tirelessly he travelled up and down the British Isles, preaching anywhere that gave him a hearing. Daily he presented the need of those without Christ. Powerfully he challenged the Christians to take up their responsibility to preach the gospel in all the world. His mouth spoke straight from his zealous heart, and his willingness to embrace sacrifice carried its own conviction. Surely his zeal and determination to obey the call of God must have had a certain poignancy to the young and able-bodied. What did they see?—a middle-aged man, none too healthy but quite prepared to be reckless in his abandonment. It preached its own message.

His daughter, Edith, wrote many years later:

There is no doubt that he was a man of extraordinary vision and compelling presence. His messages were charged with challenge, humour and emotion. But it was his realism in living out his own message that attracted those who were looking for sincerity in a world of fashionable poses.

With all his ability Studd conveyed to individuals and congregations the urgency of Dr Kumm's pleas to curb the Islamic advance. Now he needed some sign that God was endorsing his plans. When a group of businessmen came forward prepared to form a backing committee for the project, C T was greatly encouraged. The plan crystallised; he would travel alone via Khartoum and investigate the mission situation in southern Sudan. The only stipulation the committee made was that before he left he should pass a medical examination.

Was it intentional that C T left his medical examination to just three weeks before his sailing date? Was he hoping that if he failed the committee would consider it too late to abandon the venture? We are only left to wonder.

As predicated the doctor decided, 'This man is not fit to go anywhere—he should stay at home.' Although C T expected rejection it was no less a shock to him, but he wouldn't allow it to hinder his arrangements. Once he had the bit between his teeth, there was little anyone could do to turn him back. He was an impulsive man, stubborn too, and he never saw the need for any contingency plans. His natural reaction to calamity was to battle through—and that's exactly what he did.

The committee were adamant—without medical approval they would remove their support. He found that very difficult to receive, but it certainly wasn't going to change his plans. The committee, mainly close friends and associates, never quite disappeared. Willie Bradshaw continued to communicate with Studd in the Sudan and provided him with credence in the eyes of the Church Missionary Society.

C T wrote of that occasion,

> The committee refused to let me go unless I promised not to go south of Khartoum. Through the information they had received from the doctor they attempted to intimidate me that if I ventured south of Khartoum, I should never come back. On my

refusing to give the promise, they declined to help me to go, withdrawing the funds necessary for such a purpose.

The whiff of intimidation was enough to launch him into a fighting mood. Change his plans? Stay at home? Such suggestions were unthinkable.

C T was a man of huge internal resources. At a time of calamity he knew how to take hold of himself, to summon up courage and to shut his ears to every voice of accusation, doubt and fear. Studd, well acquanted with his Lord, drew strength from familiar, intimate wells. He turned to God like a well-trained servant. With all his attention focussed upon his master, he said, 'You told me to go—these circumstances haven't changed your command. I go.' Without hesitation, he told the committee, 'Gentlemen, God has called me to go and I will go. I will blaze the trail, though my grave may only becoming a stepping stone that younger men may follow.'

With only three weeks to his announced sailing date, no money and no one who believed in him, he continued with his speaking engagements as if nothing had happened. Indomitable, childlike faith that trusts and believes the word of God filled his heart. Undaunted, he rose above his circumstances because he knew that God always provides for his own will. A few days later ten pounds was pressed into his hand as he left a Sunday meeting. So certain was he that God would send the remainder required that he went straight to the shipping office and confirmed his sailing. He could not resist the temptation to telephone the committee to tell them what he had done!

The ten pounds could only start him upon his journey. Studd knew that endless expense lay ahead of him, but by using the first gift as a deposit he was sowing it like a seed of faith, confident that all he required would be provided—and so it was.

For two years he had worked and planned towards this venture. Now at its imminent launch he was again on his own. Although the family had reconciled themselves to his departure, his wife's underlying opposition remained. Why did he have to do this? Why must he go? Why at this time of life should he undertake such a journey? For her the whole event was one long trial which became his also.

Was he right stubbornly to push on against all the opposition, from the committee, friends, family and even that of his own wife, and to decide independently to go on what some considered a wild scheme? Perhaps if we had been closer to the events we too would have judged him wrong and misguided. Now with hindsight we see the full picture: mighty victories, souls won, and the routing of the powers of darkness. So much was accomplished—at a price. Studd paid the price in the hard currency of determination and obedience, ignoring those who misunderstood and maligned.

By what standard should we judge pioneers? The very fact that they are in the vanguard leading the way, requires them to be a step ahead of others in vision and thinking. Rarely will they be in tune with the expectations and attitudes of what Studd called the 'stay at home' Christian. So often the pioneer provides the irritant in relationships and situations. He is an awkward character with certain unique qualities which equip him for his task; but the same qualities, when unbridled, can be seen as huge flaws. Without the pioneer's bravado, determination and independence which is part of his make-up, nothing would be accomplished. It is only that kind of person who has the audacity to march into the devil's strongholds and defy him on his own ground.

As Charles Studd sailed out of Liverpool, complex emotions swept over him. 'Lord I delight to do your will. Whatever the opposition I will battle through. Priscilla my love—I don't want to hurt you, I love you but I must go.' Like his Master, 'he steadfastly set his face' and went on.

CHAPTER SIXTEEN

PRISCILLA ALONE

A S THE SS WARWICKSHIRE pulled away from Liverpool on December 15th, 1910, and disappeared
into the cold, grey, wintry mist, Priscilla felt
desperately alone. Charlie's life had always
been a whirl, travelling anywhere opportunity opened a door
for him. Nothing quenched his heroic zeal to save souls. So
many times she had sat alone in the evenings and watched the
embers die in the hearth as she waited for him, but this was
different. He had left in poor health and against doctor's
orders. Not one of those near and dear to him or any committee
member agreed with his going.

Priscilla and three of her daughters lived with Charlie's
mother at 2 Hyde Park Gardens. The girls were very beautiful
and at the age for 'coming out parties' and other such society
events. The bustle of family life with friends calling and visits
to be made meant Priscilla usually had someone around, but
nothing could fill the aching void that yawned in her heart.
Charlie had gone.

She had pleaded with him, but it had made no difference.
He wouldn't be persuaded, even though the committee had
written two months earlier saying they unanimously felt

Priscilla should accompany him. 'You should both go for two months or so, as far as Khartoum,' they wrote, but Charlie wouldn't hear of it. He had no intention of being restricted to such a timetable or to be exposed to the pressure of having to comply with Priscilla's wishes. Alfred Ruscoe, a missionary, later said of C T, 'He had a habit of being irritatingly right.' This turned out to be one of those occasions, but even so Priscilla could not come to terms with the situation.

Charlie had lovingly written to her on 25th November,

> I have declined to take you Priscilla darling. I simply dare not and will not . . . I cannot and will not risk your health, you are too important and necessary to me and the girls . . . you are more to me than all and I gladly though sorrowfully make the sacrifice rather than losing you my darling. God bless you . . . . My heart has ever been full of love to you and ever will be, so comfort yourself with these words and never doubt my love again . . . .

Despite such protestations Priscilla found it hard to reconcile love with his actions.

Perhaps we should bear in mind that at the age of forty-six many women are entering a rather difficult period in their lives. Their emotional and physical needs can be demanding, something husbands of Studd's ilk would hardly countenance. His advice to her was always, seek God, repent and win souls. Living as she did, I wonder what quality of spiritual fellowship was available to Priscilla? For her, their years in China had provided maximum joy and satisfaction. She would often refer to them when talking to her daughters. She had left her own missionary call and sphere of spiritual fulfilment when they returned to the comfortable, upper-class family life of Hyde Park Gardens; outwardly so fine, but in reality a spiritual desert. Life in London was a far cry from the thrill and involvement of ministry in China. Charlie usually travelled alone to his various preaching engagements, leaving

Priscilla with the girls or to visit friends and relatives. To add to her difficulties she had not enjoyed good health for some time.

Living back at Hyde Park Gardens, daily exposed to a lifestyle and expectation which was way above their means, also took its toll. The girls moved in a wealthy society but with all the embarrassment of not having sufficient money. Edith said, 'We would only have one hat between us, one day Dorothy would trim it for an occasion then another sister would dress it up for something else. We always hoped no one would notice.' Grace, the eldest, rebelled—she couldn't get away from home soon enough. The nonconformity of their lives was too hard for her to bear. She married a very wealthy older man but was sadly unhappy and soon a widow.

Such heartbreaks bear heavily upon a mother. Priscilla felt torn. How she wanted the best for her girls, but life was too complex to actually identify the best and then to convince beautiful, fun-loving daughters.

Through dozens of small unavoidable circumstances Priscilla had lost out spiritually. Every voice around her only supported her point of view. Charlie should never have gone. Convinced that she meant little or nothing to him she complained to him in her occasional letters, 'If you loved me you would not have gone. You should have taken advice, and what of your own health?' and so the arguments went on.

Even his persistent correspondence assuring her of his devotion and telling of encounters with God did nothing to relieve her state. Charlie, so unhappy with her too infrequent, short letters, accused her of no longer loving him and feared she would even become his enemy. On February 23rd, 1911, he wrote, 'What's happened to you? No longer are you the one who would say, 'Praise the Lord,' and, 'Rejoice always,' and, 'Thy will be done.' You've lost your first love and got caught up in the snares of life.' She was so obviously burdened for many things.

Sole responsibility for their daughters, financial constraint, poor health, loneliness and disappointment made Priscilla a very unhappy lady who urgently needed a new encounter with the Lord.

She had written to Charlie asking for a home of their own. She found living in the centre of his family too difficult. Their daughters were making various arrangements and friendships with wealthy, titled people, and problems began to arise from the tempting worldly interests that were paraded before the girls. The situation became fraught; they hadn't the money to engage in that extravagant kind of lifestyle, and besides Charles was unhappy with the direction his daughters were taking. When 'coming out' parties were mentioned Charlie wrote, 'And what would my father have thought?' That manner of affluent, luxurious society was a source of pain to C T Studd. He wrote to Priscilla,

> For the time being we will be better off out of it. Of course I know I've committed the unpardonable sin of being poor and having made myself poor. No doubt I've been a trial and a trouble to them but I won't be so much more. Well, we can't imagine what it's going to be, but we'll have a home somewhere on the earth with Jesus. He shall have to choose our inheritance for us and we're committed to show the world and Christians that our hearts have always been in the battlefield and not in the luxuries of home life.

In the middle of all these painful trials and pressures Charlie wrote to his wife, 'Will you take the girls to the Salvation Army. I want them to come out as red-hot fighting soldiers!'

CHAPTER SEVENTEEN

A CONTINUING SACRIFICE

THE CONSEQUENCES OF giving away his fortune continued to cause painful and embarrassing repercussions. During the six months that Studd spent in the Sudan, financial pressures at home prompted concerned attempts by family and friends to provide for his wife and daughters. He felt humiliated by what his brothers considered self-imposed poverty. In a depressed moment Studd said, 'It would be better to settle in Africa and never return.'

Despite such difficult episodes in Studd's life, he experienced the Lord to be no man's debtor. God certainly provided for C T Studd's extensive travels and the maintenance of his family, but problems arose when the money available failed to maintain them in a similar standard to that which they had forsaken. His family, particularly his mother, continuously provided for him. What an embarrassment! He lived with his mother and ate at her lavish table, but at the same time he was shunned by many family members and treated as the poor relation. C T found their misunderstanding and disdain a constant thorn in the flesh; it made him cautious with strangers. He said, 'I wouldn't want to sponge.'

His daughters felt their lack of money most keenly. It was assumed that people moving in their strata of society had private finances. Studd, aware of all these pressures upon his children, advised their mother to 'Steer them towards the Buxton's, a good family with the right Christian values.' Studd admired them because they shared his zeal for the mission field and, although they had money, did not participate in the wordly social scene. Barclay Buxton, the founder of the Japan Evangelistic Band, came from a similar family to C T Studd's, but he had not been led to part with his share of the family inheritance. He believed the money belonged to his children as much as to himself.

C T Studd had given away a fortune, but God had promised in his word, 'Give and it will be given unto you.' Over the years more than a fortune returned to the Studd family and continues to flow into the mission he founded. The work has expanded worldwide and is still financed by the gifts of God's people in response to believing prayer.

Studd shone out as a challenge and an example to his generation. His initial sacrificial gift stood as a stark symbol of his total abandonment to God. Some called his reckless generosity 'fanatical', but for Studd it was only his reasonable service.

He continued all his years to live with the same heart attitude. All he was and had belonged to the Lord. When the call to Africa came and he heard the challenge again, he wrote to his wife, 'Seldom in a life do two people have the opportunity to forsake all twice, but we are being offered this privilege. Let us grasp it with both hands.' See the magnitude of his heart as he departed to Africa without his wife, an event that gave his critics plenty of ammunition. Tongues wagged as they always do; it is part of the persecution experienced by those who wholly follow the Lord.

Today, with so much teaching on family life, it is hard to conceive of a man leaving his wife in this manner, but can we judge? We didn't receive the call, nor can we enter into the complexity of their particular dealings with God. A passion for souls held CT's heart. God had spoken to him; he must take the news of salvation to pagan Africa. Driven with a powerful determination, he refused to be deflected by the cost. He strengthened his inner man with steel, denied himself, refused the pain and obeyed. Perhaps not every detail of the way in which he stayed apart from his wife for so long was correct, but no one can deny his complete sincerity. Together they had the opportunity to embrace total surrender a second time. God has set them forth as a timeless example of those who followed the Lord whatever the price.

The criticism of Christian people became the most painful part of the cross the Studds had to bear. The disdain of family members, the accusation of failing to provide, coupled with the unkindness of dozens of misinformed people who accused Charles Studd of outrageous neglect of his wife, added together to make him something of a contradiction and a source of puzzlement. It ensured that only those with the eye of faith would applaud; the remainder would vilify.

Fame, wealth, position, worldy prospects—all were counted as rubbish to gain Christ. Then family, wife, companionship, home comforts, grandchildren and so much more besides, were deliberately put upon the altar of sacrifice. Not one only to talk about sacrifice, he actually paid the price and blazed a trail which thousands down the years have followed in their own unique way.

His life is the most powerful rebuke to half-hearted Christians. Who could sit at ease when an asthmatic, plagued with numerous other ailments and at the age when most settle down, was willing to go, alone if necessary, to the heart of Africa for the sake of Christ and lost souls?

He didn't need to open his mouth; his life preached its own message. Utter sincerity and transparent attitudes character-ised this rugged gentleman. He was the ultimate doer of

God's word. He couldn't countenance saying or singing one thing and doing the opposite. Regardless of the cost he would obey.

When he wrote *The Chocolate Soldier* he graphically portrayed his own heart:

> Every true Christian is a Soldier of Christ—a hero 'par excellence!' Braver than the bravest—scorning the soft seductions of peace and her oft-repeated warnings against hardship, disease, danger and death, whom he counts among his bosom friends.

He didn't care a 'brass button' as he would often say, for the opinions of men. He was a 'real hero untainted by the fear of man.' He wrote:

> Learn to scorn the praise of men,
> Learn to lose with God;
> Jesus won the world thro' shame!
> And beckons us his road.

CHAPTER EIGHTEEN

DEATH TO HIMSELF

BEFORE FOLLOWING C T into his Khartoum expedition, let us look once more at that painful moment when he sailed alone from Liverpool, but this time from *his* perspective.

Standing on the upper deck alone, Charlie's eyes remained fixed on Priscilla as the ship eased its way out of the dock. Both their hearts struck the same chord of anguish at their parting. He steadied his with the knowledge of the call of God and reinforced it with the steel of determination. He had heard the invitation to go; for him there was no alternative— he must go. Obedience always brings strength. Priscilla had heard no such word; instead her mind raced through a multitude of hurt feelings tinged with anger and bitterness. What was she going to do?

As her lonely, cold figure passed from view Charlie, powerless to help her, went below to the comfort of his cabin where he wrote, 'Darling, this is going to be a big work. We need to get to know our Captain better.' He continued to assure her of his love.

On the 15th of December, 1910, he wrote,

I feel Jesus says to each one of us two just now, "Come into a desert place apart and rest awhile with me..." You must now rest in the arms of Jesus, you are safe there. I leave you there. Nestle close to his heart for he loves you dearly. Whisper back your love to him.

What began as an exciting expedition had turned into a painful emotional trauma. The only remedy for healing was to embrace a new depth of suffering and death to himself. He now found himself walking out to do God's will alone, without even the approval of his wife. He wrote at that time, 'Nothing was more costly,' but with characteristic determination and zeal he refused the luxury of indulging his own feelings and decided to do God's will.

He wrote to his wife,

Perhaps at last you will realise how I love you when I tell you my going to Khartoum has cost me myself, and all the ignoring of what folks will say about you not going.... This venture has got to be a venture of faith and heroism and it is well to begin it there.... He will see us through this, and much more. He will enable us both to do the biggest work of our lives for Christ these coming years.

When the Lord takes his children through such experiences he knows exactly how to sustain them. The psalmist could write,

Yea, though I walk through the valley of the shadow of death, I will fear no evil: for thou art with me; thy rod and thy staff they comfort me. Thou preparest a table before me in the presence of mine enemies: thou anointest my head with oil; my cup runneth over (Ps 23:4–5).

The Lord sustained his servant, and that night alone in his cabin God spoke to him. 'This trip is not merely for the

Sudan, it is for the whole unevangelised world.' Such a momentous revelation found a lodging place in his heart, despite its sheer impossibility. The cry of the whole unevangelised world had been spelt out in words of anguish at the 1910 World Missionary Conference, and now God spoke to him again.

The concept was too large for the immediate but was never allowed to die. As Studd carefully put himself in the way of the Lord, regardless of endless opposition, the vision grew and grew over the next years till it filled his thinking, writing and praying.

The committee at home originally had only sanctioned a visit as far as Khartoum. To go further south was considered too great a risk to health. Now free from their restrictions, C T Studd realised that to get experience and understanding of the unevangelised regions south of Khartoum he would have to travel and see for himself.

I doubt he gave much thought to the niceties of consulting with the committee before later moving off on his investigation. Studd was an independent at heart who tried hard to work with committees but who refused to be guided or controlled by them. In his opinion the man on the front line was the one to make the decisions.

When William Bradshaw, the secretary of the committee, a long-standing family friend, insisted Studd should return home to be present to share the London farewell meeting for Dr Kumm, Studd refused and continued with his plans to investigate southern Sudan. Dependence upon the Lord for his financial supply, the personal nature of the call upon his life and his own determination to see it accomplished, encouraged his sense of independence from men.

Whilst waiting in Khartoum, Studd, never one to be idle, found plenty of preaching opportunities among the British Army. He had a mission to the men of the Yorkshire regiment and had the satisfaction of seeing souls saved. An army captain wrote, 'Where can I find Studd's text from last night? I want to mark it. His address was magnificent and appealed to all the men I've spoken to in the most marked way,'

Besides the soldiers there was a large community of expatriate British residing there for a variety of reasons. He lectured to them on China and preached in the CMS church, but he was none too enamoured with their less than hearty spiritual life. He wrote home, 'I disliked their proper lifeless faces.' He thought they were saying on the inside, 'What on earth are you doing coming here to wake us up!'

The Europeans had created a very pleasant life, with servants galore removing almost every inconvenience. Thus freed they spent their time in idle pastimes, talking and pleasure-seeking. Studd would have none of their picnics and parties. He expressed utter contempt for their frivolous ways. Sickened by the staleness of formal Christianity and rejecting the worldly expatriate style of living, Studd wrote, 'I had a good time in Matthew 6, especially verse 19, "Do not lay up for yourselves treasures on earth, where moth and rust consume and where thieves break in and steal."' Then he counselled his wife, 'Do not be anxious concerning money.'

From wherever we catch glimpses of this man's life, regardless of circumstances, difficulties, emotional upheavals or contentions, he is hard at work. His output was prodigious—the result of a disciplined spirit. He wrote home, 'Got up at 5.15 am, had a good read till breakfast at 8.45, and since then have been glued to my desk writing letters and reports.' One who observed him wrote, 'He spends his time absorbed with his maps, plans, blue books or interviewing some government official.'

There in Khartoum he withdrew into the Lord and his word. With work filling his days he shut out the irksome, pseudo-religious life that secretly disgusted him. He could find no grace to excuse those employed supposedly as missionaries, but who spent their days in anything but spreading the gospel; neither for those who believed anything but the 'plain black and white truth of the Bible.'

Studd found his stay in Khartoum irritating and freely talked at one point of his visit 'being a waste of time'. He experienced great difficulty in collecting hard facts about the missionary needs of the area. The expectations of the missionaries and the results they achieved were far removed from his ideals—he began to doubt the usefulness of the information he would obtain. None of this helped when news from home rarely brought happiness. Indeed both Charlie and his wife were going through a painful trial.

*   *   *

Arrangements were eventually completed after weeks of delay, and, ignoring the strong letters from home, Studd set out on a 900 mile trek through southern Sudan into the region of Bahr-el-Ghazal, near the head-waters of the Nile, and the borders of the Belgian Congo. His companions were Bishop Gwynne of Khartoum and Archdeacon Shaw of the Church Missionary Society. They were to visit mission stations en route and complete a survey of mission effectiveness.

The Home Committee had good reason to object to Studd travelling in this region. It was renowned for malaria and sleeping sickness, and already a letter had reached home saying, 'Mr Studd is not looking too well and there is plenty of sickness in the area... but I don't think your husband is likely to be influenced by other people's anxieties.' No, certainly not! C T Studd never gave them half a thought. Convinced that God had commissioned his journey, he was prepared to travel and trust the Lord to keep him in health and bring him back safely.

Before he had set foot upon African soil C T had soaked

himself in the extensive need of the continent. The twenty-six most vulnerable unevangelised tribes were more than names to him. As he launched out on the tour, he went armed with lists of facts. He had acquainted himself with the difficulties of evangelising over such vast distances and among scattered populations. He knew there were over 500 different languages and some 300 additional dialects in the region. The obstruction to missionary work by colonial powers was proverbial, so he planned to make contacts and good relationships. The greater accessibility of the scattered villages because of modern transportation had made it easier for the Muslim as well as the Christian, but the Muslim was arriving there first.

How could Studd rest, and how could a man of his character sit patiently by while, in his opinion, the missionaries were 'twiddling their thumbs'?

The party travelled by mule with donkeys to carry their supplies, equipment and numerous helpers. Charles Studd became convinced that he couldn't work with the CMS but, looking at the need, decided that by a slight expansion of their own work they could more effectively cover the area. Disillusioned by the sparseness of the population, his eyes strayed further west.

Bishop Gwynne wrote home to Willie Bradshaw on July 31st, 1911,

We only discovered 20,000 souls in the whole Lado enclave. The sphere open to missionary work is Bahr-el-Ghazal and the Lado enclave. There is a tribe called Azandis — these people present the best opportunity for witness. There are other smaller tribes. There's great difficulty in undertaking the evangelisation of these people because of the small numbers and the large variety of languages, yet . . . . the Muslims are there proselytising.

The same letter continues that the Bishop hoped the Sudan Evangelical Mission, the first name adopted by Studd for his mission, would take up these smaller opportunities, whilst leaving the CMS to deal with the Azandis as they already had experience amongst them. The final report goes on to say, 'The Azandis spread across the Sudan border into French and Belgian territory, there are large numbers of them, all unevangelised. They are the ones which need to be followed up.' Obviously from that point on the seeds were sown in Studd's heart to cross that border if at all possible. He wanted to be among the greater concentrations of people. The Azandis were also known as the Niam Niams, the name he gave to his home which became the headquarters of the mission. At that time Studd was under the impression that it would not be easy for a British person to enter the Belgian Congo, so his plans still majored upon the Sudan.

Studd, the visionary, went by 'feel'. He didn't have to come up to anyone's expectations or follow a pre-announced path. When it became obvious a change of direction was required he had no problem apparently changing his mind. Although the purpose of this journey was to explore the mission potential of southern Sudan, his eye naturally strayed into any open door of the Lord. He didn't need to apologise for a change of plans—such didn't exist in his thinking because he was following the Lord.

As the little convoy made its way back to Khartoum, Studd was more than pleased that it was over. He hadn't enjoyed the tour. What he had seen only enhanced his desire to bring in missionaries who would tackle the task on a warlike footing. Aware that the enemy of men's souls was firmly entrenched, he feared the present missionary activity would only Christianise the people. He wanted converts who would be red-hot firebrands for Jesus to make an all-out onslaught against the powers of darkness. He wrote at this time to Willie Bradshaw, 'God works with insignificant minorities like Gideon's 300, not the 3,000. Let us be God's peculiar people; such spells absolute fidelity to God's word.'

Had he eventually worked with the CMS, he would have been a square peg in a round hole—a revolutionary standing up in the children's meeting singing at the top of his voice 'Onward Christian soldiers' when everyone else was singing 'Gentle Jesus meek and mild'.

His health had been good on the safari so he refused to be carried and walked most of the way. During every available resting moment he had written copious letters to encourage his wife and notes to share with the committee at home. He detailed the terrain, the weather, the availability of water and food, as well as the people and their movements.

He was a compassionate man. The suffering of the pack of donkeys on the journey troubled him and he wrote home one day, 'From 4 pm—7 pm I dressed the sores of innumerable donkeys besides doctoring several men.' Throughout his life C T avoided doctors, and he treated himself and anyone else who was willing. Before the party could return the tsetse fly killed twenty-nine of their thirty donkeys during the two-and-a-half-month trek.

He was pleased to return to Khartoum but unfortunately was again delayed, this time struck down with a severe attack of malaria. Critically ill, he lay in Khartoum perhaps wondering what he should tell interested parties when he arrived home. A journey that the committee had intended should take two months had taken six. Back in England Studd recuperated during the summer of 1911, then reassessed the visit and the means by which he could accomplish the great task.

CHAPTER NINETEEN

DETERMINED AGAINST ALL ODDS

WITH HIS PASSION for the salvation of the unevangelised thoroughly charged, C T was on the move again, preaching, informing, cajoling and challenging in his own inimitable way. His heartfelt messages overflowed with zest and humour, ending always on a note of compulsion. 'There's an unevangelised world out there. Do something about it and do it now!' But his call so often fell upon cold, unresponsive hearts.

Studd could still draw a large audience in the universities; his cricketing career had not been forgotten, and his adventurous escapades for Christ appealed to the young people. A capacity crowd filled the great Guildhall in Cambridge, and I'm sure the dons who sat in the front rows wished halfway through the meeting that they were anywhere else but there. The blistering message stirred up plenty of antagonism. As soon as they were able they left, in silent disapproval.

C T Studd's abrasive talk didn't deter the undergraduates from inviting him to speak to them again. They were intrigued by his audacity. He would take the lion in his den! Who would travel to cannibal tribes with him? The element of adventure appealed to the young, and with great interest they questioned him. He looked for response—who would go to Africa, who would trust God to supply all his needs? His daughter Edith said, 'When they were slow to respond, his sharp riposte came, "No need to tell me what you are thinking. You are saying, 'Here I am Lord but send my sister!'"'

One of the fascinated young men listening to C T was Alfred Buxton, the second son of Barclay Buxton, who was a friend of the Studd family. Alfred, an undergraduate, intended becoming a medical doctor. In 1910, before C T Studd's expedition to the Sudan, Dr Kumm preached in Cambridge, and Alfred had heard him with great interest. He would have dearly loved to abandon his university studies and volunteer for immediate missionary service. In a letter, the nineteen-year-old Alfred wrote, 'Kumm is trying to get a band of men together. Mr Studd is going . . . I wish my exams were done and I could go too.' So he expressed his boyish enthusiasm.

When Mr Studd himself presented the same need of the numerous tribes across Africa every responsive nerve was alert in Alfred. He was a godly young man who simply wanted to serve God.

When he broke the news to his parents that he wished to travel with C T Studd on his next journey to Africa, the family's response was cool to say the least. No one would endorse his plans. Each person consulted said, 'Complete your training, qualify, then see what the Lord is saying.' Wisely left to ponder his own decision, Alfred came to the conclusion that God wanted him to accompany Studd. He had another reason for his affinity to Studd—for two years letters had passed between himself and Edith, Charles' daughter. We know Edith had a special place in his heart. Perhaps this influenced Alfred's decision making.

Studd had an incredible ability to relate to young men. He

was a man's man, always assured of an excellent reception in the universities. He spoke success in the terms young men most readily understood. Twenty-four initially responded to Studd's call, though less than half that number eventually went.

Gathering an eager group of young men who were ready to take on Africa was simple in comparison to providing a solid foundation from which they could be sent out, supported in prayer and adequately financed. C T Studd never took offerings for the work and did little to mention the need in public, except to declare his trust in God who would supply all his needs.

In between speaking engagements Studd was feeling his way into relationships that would form a sending base for the new mission he dreamed of establishing. He began to identify the type of mission he wanted and the kind of missionary he could accept. His disappointment with the CMS work in the Sudan, which he didn't like to mention publicly, surely prompted him to clarify the doctrinal principles for his future work.

He wrote to his new committee, which now called itself the Eastern Sudan Evangelical Mission Committee, saying, 'It is necessary for us to state our case and the foundational principles for this mission.' Then he enlarged upon these five points which he later called five smooth stones:

1. Absolute faith in the deity of each person of the Trinity

2. Absolute belief in the full inspiration of the Old and New Testament Scriptures

3. Vow to know and to preach none other save Jesus Christ and him crucified

4. Obedience to Christ's command to love all who love the Lord Jesus, sincerely, without respect of persons, and to love all men

5. Absolute faith in the will, power and providence of God
   to meet our every need in his service

Soon afterwards it appears that the committee was disbanded, and Studd looked for another possible alliance. Studd's understanding of the missionary needs of the region were of interest to AIM, the African Inland Mission. This led to some dialogue with their committee, but in usual Studd fashion nothing was finalised until the last moment. Probably he was waiting to see if any other more promising door opened to him before forming too close an alliance with AIM.

So much uncertainty could hardly have encouraged the Buxton family to agree to Alfred's venture. For eight months Alfred agonised over his decision. Every objection was put before him, but the call to go wouldn't leave him. Finally on his 21st birthday he asked God to give him, 'Just one more revelation of his will.' Two texts from the morning sermon spoke to him.

The first text was, 'Do thy diligence to come shortly unto me' (2 Tim 4:9), which was followed by, 'But I have prayed for thee, that thy faith fail not...' (Lk 22:32).

In the evening he went to hear his father preach. His text was that great word to hesitant Gideon, 'Go in this thy might...' (Judg 6:14). It came like a sword thrust into Alfred's heart; God had spoken. His father became God's final mouthpiece. That night Alfred told his father who listened with bowed head—he too recognised the word of God.

These events were no less unsettling to Priscilla and their two remaining unmarried daughters. It was obvious to Priscilla that no amount of persuasion was going to have any influence upon her Charlie. She recognised only too clearly the call of God was upon his life. He would not be deflected by her, committees, the opinions of men or the direct onslaught of the enemy. He would go to Africa. The opposition only stirred him up to a greater fight and determination.

Certainly the family went through a time of great anguish and Priscilla a period of deep soul-searching. Edith said,

> To me my father's goings-on were quite incomprehensible. As a family we had had enough adversity. To go out and seek more was sheer madness, but his life and message must have reached my subconscious, for when I came to go to Africa for a much lesser motive, I found myself able to do so.

Again Priscilla pleaded for a home of their own. Then Charlie saw a house that looked the very thing at a wonderfully reasonable price. He said,

> I felt I had to have that house and it became such an obsession that at last my wife said to me, "Oh never mind the house: you don't get any sleep these nights thinking and praying about that old place. You go along [referring to his journey to Africa] and we will manage somehow."

God saw their need, and with a loan from his mother, which she turned into a gift, they purchased 17 Highland Road in Norwood, London.

The house was then furnished by little miracles, mainly from the auction rooms, and cost next to nothing. One day Studd wandered into the open back door of a shop and found himself in a large furniture auction. He said, 'I saw things being knocked down at the most ridiculous prices. Before leaving I had invested in a walnut library chair, upholstered in Morocco, for which I paid the fancy price of fifteen shillings.' In a similar fashion they were able to carpet the house from top to bottom and find furniture to suit all their needs. God was good.

No doubt this timely answer to prayer helped Priscilla to come to a better frame of mind, although she could not entirely accept Charlie's behaviour. Her need was deep;

nothing short of a miraculous revelation of God's will for both of their lives could carry her through the days, weeks and months—she never dreamt it would be years—that lay ahead of her.

Time was getting short, Studd was impatient to sail. The Cambridge men needed decisions. Under whose auspices were they to go? Plans still lingered around the Sudan, but Studd's ideas were not locked into that nation. He had seen the readiness over the border in the Congo and, as the saga of their journey was to unfold, the Congo presented itself as the perfect field of opportunity.

Discussions with the AIM suddenly came to the point of action. The prospective Cambridge missionaries had dwindled to Buxton, Rampley, Morris and Batstone. On November 12th, 1912, Studd applied to join the AIM along with the young men. His application form was completed with some jesting, and his medical report form tells us nothing of his true state. He filled it in himself, without taking any point seriously. When asked for his pastor's name and church affinity he was equally vague, writing, 'The Lord Jesus Christ and his church.'

Studd was intimately involved with the formation of the AIM Committee, and some of his own close supporters— even Mr Barclay Buxton—were included in its number. Studd knew exactly what kind of mission he wanted. He had already carefully identified acceptable doctrine and practice and did not intend to compromise. Soon he was sitting uncomfortably with the AIM, and they with him. The USA branch of AIM had their own financial policy and constitution which at one point Studd accepted but on later reflection rejected. He wanted the British branch of AIM to be independent of America. Talk ranged around amending the constitution; Studd suggested far-reaching changes. He virtually wished to establish a new mission; but no conclusion was reached before he and his party sailed.

Fearing that when the issues were again debated his views would not carry the day, Studd wrote a letter resigning from the mission and left it with his spokesmen. It was to be presented if the committee reaffirmed a constitution and financial policy that was contrary to his own views.

Studd, a member of the first English council of AIM, accepted as a missionary and then appointed field director, sailed as leader of the AIM missionary party on January 13th, 1913, to East Africa for work in the Belgian Congo.

His short career with AIM ended on March 13th, 1913— but before we elaborate upon that let us take one more look at Priscilla during these last hectic days.

CHAPTER TWENTY

A NEW PRISCILLA

THE DAY BEFORE he sailed C T Studd sat in his own home, at his own desk, and wrote a letter to his dear wife.

I hope you are resting and feeling better [she was again very unwell]. God is putting upon us an amazing honour, he seldom gives anyone the chance to sacrifice all the second time. Wonders will follow of his love and power. Our God shall bless you darling; may he speak through us to his people in these days! The sacrifice of his real children is the ear-trumpet which enables his deaf and sleeping people to hear. May he speak and speak very loudly through us to his people in the churches and to those outside.

The following day he wrote again, this time from a hotel in Dover just before he sailed. 'Dear darling Cilla, you have always been and always shall be my darling, and all the more now because you have so sacrificed for Jesus sake. I fairly laugh at the idea of the huge reward you shall get.'

Despite months of uncertainty when Priscilla only faced a fearful future, she fought her way through into an amazing spiritual victory where God met her. At an age when most women are comfortable grannies, Priscilla found the front line of spiritual warfare ranged right through her own soul. Would God provide for her? How would she manage the home by herself? Could she cope with the loneliness, feeling so cut off when mail took at least six weeks? Could she trust God in her own weakness—what if she couldn't find strength to run her home? And Charlie wasn't fit—how would he manage when he was sick? With acute pain she brought every area of doubt and crying need to God. Deliberately she cast all her anxieties upon Jesus and found him trustworthy.

In the deepest parts of her being she acquiesced to God— there was nothing she could change but her own attitudes, so she did and peace rushed in.

Priscilla couldn't hide her doubts about CT's previous journey. She had discovered herself at variance with him again and again, especially when she found her security undermined. Could she trust her husband when he refused guidance and counsel, preferring to press on in his own determined, independent way? Relinquishing all such doubts, she let the Spirit of God minister to her heart.

Writing from Suez on the 7th February, Charlie said,

> My heart's love to you my darling. It is a great glory that I can so utterly trust you. What would I do were you not at home, I do not know. It is a comfort and joy that I cannot describe. I shall always write my heart out to you.

Her radical change of attitude brought release and joy to him. Never had he questioned his decision to go—he would go regardless of her opinion and, it appears, regardless of her state of health, but certainly his leaving became so much sweeter now he had confidence that she would co-operate.

*　　　*　　　*

Nothing was ever plain sailing with such a husband. He had a habit of setting his life on a collision course, and the next mighty impact was only a few weeks away.

He was still en route to Africa when he posted a letter from Suez saying, 'The more I pray and the more I think, the more I am determined to have Jesus the Captain of this expedition and no other.' He was already entertaining serious doubts about continuing with AIM. He went on to say, 'I feel sure henceforth our route to our work will be from the Congo mouth and up the River Congo to Stanleyville. That will aid our independence of America more than ever.' He was refer- ring to the American AIM. Then he went on to say,

> Don't fear for me, I am devoted to Jesus and I care not a fig for my reputation. I shall go straight as a die no matter what the cost. I've paid the price in full and shall go through with everything. I'm sure every cross will only bring more power, and the spread of the glorious name and cause of Christ. It is Jesus only I see and trust. God shall bring us out into a wealthy place if we are but faithful unto death. I mean to be so, fear not.

But I'm sure Priscilla did fear when she received such letters. She knew only too well his inclination to make impulsive decisions. He could be rash.

As could only be expected, the council of AIM in London ratified their constitution and financial policy. The minutes of that council meeting record, 'It became evident from the admissions of Studd's friends that it was probable that he would work satisfactorily on his own lines and independently of control.' Studd's letter of resignation was produced and a cable sent to him and to each of the party now in Mombasa. Unfortunately such upheavals do not occur without acrimony, but it must be said that at first, both AIM and the newly formed Heart of Africa Mission, as Studd named his new enterprise, never exposed their differences in public, and in every way endeavoured to smooth over a stormy episode.

Each one of the party had personally to decide his own future. Morris, Batstone and Rampley all remained with AIM. Alfred Buxton, not liking to be caught up in such a painful affair, wrote a 'lovely letter' of loyalty to Studd, who told his wife, 'He says he shall stick to me while my heart is to do God's will, which he knows to be the case.' Alfred wrote to the others that he was joined to God, not to the mission, nor men, nor Studd. Alfred's loyalty greatly touched C T Studd.

The division of the party posed huge problems. First of all their baggage was jointly crated, then they both intended travelling in the same direction, and, most embarrassing for Studd, a number of the places designated to provide them with hospitality and assistance on their way were AIM stations.

Studd in the midst of the whirlwind of events in Nairobi wrote copious letters to his wife complaining about the situation and stoutly defending himself. In typical masculine fashion he was able to express all his hot feelings in one paragraph and completely change the subject in his next. Despite the general content of his letters, every one included many expressions of his tender feelings for his wife. At one time she complained that he had always been undemonstrative and cool in his behaviour to her, yet his letters revealed a warm, loving heart. Most probably his mind was always so actively involved in the strategy and ministry of evangelism that he rarely gave himself the treat of just relaxing and enjoying his wife. The quote from this letter shows just how entwined were his attitudes of loving his wife and loving the Lord:

Good-bye my own sweet love. I love you more than ever for giving me up to God and we shall yet surely meet again for our very sweetest time on earth. Our giving up ourselves again to Jesus has, I believe, spoken very very loudly to the Christians at home. Folks at home are sick of words, they want to see deeds. So does everybody. Deeds mean reality. Words are such soft things. Away with all religious confectionery of today.

He signs himself, 'Love from your own precious husband.'

There were no pastel shades in his character; every trait was dominant. He loved God with all his heart; he would serve him with every ounce of his being. Whilst he had breath he would do everything in his ability to drive Christians to do the will of God, he would fight the devil on every front, he was ruthless against the flesh, and so we could go on... an ardent lover of God, but not the most comfortable person to live with!

It must be remembered that Priscilla hardly fitted the usual mould for ladies of that era. Her life had followed anything but the normal course of events. She too, loved God with all her heart and had decided to serve him with every ounce of her energy. Like her husband she had gambled everything to follow Christ, and with a similar gritty determination she had laid down her life to follow her Lord. Her sacrifices were different but equally costly, though sometimes less easy to discern because they lacked the exotic or adventurous dimension.

Only a wife who had developed her own intimate access to God could face many of the hardships that relentlessly pushed in upon Priscilla. Charles Studd was not alone in his second opportunity to sacrifice all for God. There on the altar sharing in this heavenly transaction was Priscilla. It was one thing for her to gladly release Charles to the work of the Lord, but a vastly different affair to deliberately lay down her own feelings, emotions and hopes. She had to forfeit her personal, normal, wifely expectations for support and security. Like a widow she lost the 'other half of herself', and had to manage alone without the intimacy of the marriage relationship which was so much a part of her.

Priscilla also knew how to be ruthless with herself. Her indomitable spirit drew deeper into God. The life-springs of her developed prayer life watered her thirsty soul. She would overcome.

We read in Romans 4:19 that Abraham faced the fact that his body was as good as dead. Priscilla walked in the footsteps of that giant of faith. Although hindered by a heart condition she refused to have it dictate to her way of life. She took authority over her sick body in the name of Jesus and put herself—heart, soul and body—into the work of God to support her husband in his great mission.

The words Sir Herbert Edwards wrote to his friend John Nicholson almost two centuries ago could have been written by Studd: 'I cannot tell you how good it is for our best purposes to be helped by a noble wife, who loves you better than all the men and women but God better than you.'

CHAPTER TWENTY—ONE

PAYING THE PRICE TO ENTER THE LAND

WHAT A STRANGE PAIR Studd and Buxton must have appeared: one a man of fifty-two years, full of life's experience, living in a body well worn by toil; his companion, only twenty-one, earnest, eager and so sincere, still touched with the naïvety of youth. 'One too old and one too young.'

Before embarking upon their long journey, Studd preached once more in Nairobi with his accustomed anointing and power. He happened to be part of the congregation when, without warning, he was invited to preach. After the event the church magazine reported, 'Some people had been deliberately prejudiced against Mr Studd. The word of God soon disarmed them. We found his address at communion wonderfully pointed and telling: one of the most beautiful I have ever heard from anyone.'

Wherever C T Studd went he was in demand as a speaker. He possessed an ability to present old truths in a fresh way and powerfully to apply the commands of Scripture without compromise. He made no attempt to wrap painful truth up in pretty words. The word of God came stinging home on target from every quarter, leaving the hearers convicted and

challenged. When he preached he didn't supply extra knowledge to add to knowledge, but rather commands of God to
be obeyed by the power of the Spirit. Not the kind of speaker
you invited if you wanted a word to tickle your ears! It's little
wonder that not all were his friends.

Next day the two men took the train from Nairobi heading
west to Lake Victoria. They transferred to a steamer, then
another train and another steamer—five altogether—
followed by a motor journey to Masindi, a small CMS station
in Uganda where they arrived on April 11th. Masindi marked
the end of the road and, for the forseeable future, the end of
civilisation of that kind. Their next destination was Lake
Albert, three days walk away. But that was to become the
least of their trials.

A cable had arrived from Alfred's father. Hungry for news
the young man quickly tore it open. Its contents turned out
to be a powerful assault upon Alfred Buxton's call to Africa.
Carefully he read, 'Cannot consent you two going interior
alone.' The fire was heated seven times hotter; his decision
was again put to the trial. His family naturally were alarmed
by stories of the danger that lay ahead and felt strengthened
in their argument by letters from missionaries in Africa who
said it was most inadvisable for Alfred to continue on this
'wildcat scheme'. He was completely inexperienced and C T
Studd too old and precarious in health.

Four months had passed since they left home, plenty of
time for the glamour of the journey to evaporate in the face of
stark realities—trials, hardships, divisions, doubts and
insecurities.

Alfred had every reason to soberly consider returning—
after all he had become engaged to be married to Edith Studd
on the eve of his departure. He could make so many people
happy by turning back.

Alfred Buxton proved himself to be no mere follower of
men but a true son of God. 'I'm going on.' His decision was

reaffirmed and the strong temptation overcome. A man of God and a courageous pioneer were welded more strongly into the spearhead of God's invasion into the heart of Africa. His reply said, 'Must go on. Fear nothing. Ps 105:12–15,' which reads:

> When they were but a few in number, few indeed, and strangers in it, they wandered from nation to nation, from one kingdom to another. He allowed no-one to oppress them; for their sake he rebuked kings; "Do not touch my anointed ones; do my prophets no harm" (NIV).

With the cable dispatched, Studd thankfully emerged from his own trial. He had battled it out in prayer, not wishing to influence so serious a decision. Now he could feel even more confident—he had the right man as companion. Alfred's father replied in his next letter, 'I'm glad you're going on and am sure it is right. I'm glad that I have a son who is prepared to risk something for the name of the Lord.'

Norman Grubb comments in his biography on Alfred Buxton,

> Right up to the zero hour the young adventurer of faith was given the Gideon test, "Whosoever is fearful and afraid, let him return," and rightly given it through those whose duty it was to counsel prudence and, "Try the spirits whether they are of God." By such means does God test, reveal, and toughen his true soldiers. Alfred was maturing from child to man of God.

The next day they pressed on, but only after the unfortunate loss of a tent. Fire had gutted it during a vain attempt to drive out an invasion of ants.

I wonder what mixed emotions filled C T Studd's heart as he looked across Lake Albert to the far shore—there before him lay their first glimpse of the Congo. Against many odds, they had come this far—God had supplied health and strength and provided for all their needs, even if sometimes he didn't provide in the way they would have chosen.

Together both men bowed their heads and prayed. Buxton said, 'Looking across the lake to the hills beyond, shrouded in mist, it is like viewing the walls encircling our Jericho.' They laid their countless problems out before the Lord. 'Father give us favour with the government officials, help us to get entry into the land, show us where to go—direct our paths.'

The AIM had sent missionaries into the region just six months previously and had established a mission station at the landing stage on the Congo side of the lake. Would they now help or hinder the progress of two lone men intending to establish a separate mission?

While Studd had been in Nairobi, with cables flying backwards and forwards between himself and London, it had been agreed that AIM and Studd should amicably divide the work among the Azandis. Studd now wondered how that would actually happen. Relationships had deteriorated with countless misunderstandings and accusations.

Awake early the next day, trusting solely in the Lord, they boarded their last steamer for the gentle journey across a lake as large as an inland sea. The Lord went before them and wonderfully opened the way. Despite their unaffiliated state they were allowed to enter, and they received hospitality for a few days from the missionaries at Mahagi.

To African eyes Studd must have looked an old man, though his mental faculties were anything but old. Few Europeans of his age survived the special rigours of uncivilised tropical life. His grasp of the region was comprehensive; he had a good understanding of the most advisable areas of opportunity. Once it was clear that some delay would ensue before their trunks and books arrived, they decided to dismantle their tents by the lake and move south.

With their kit packed again and porters gathered, the trek to Kilo began. For the next eight days the two companions cycled and walked in the company of Mr Gribble of the AIM. As they walked away from Mahagi, they entered regions where no Protestant missions existed. The darkness of heathenism had never been disturbed. The ruling spirits controlling the district held their prey captive with a tyrannical grip.

Stories abounded giving plenty of substance to the fear of travelling in the region. Recently a white trader had been killed by a poisoned arrow. The white man was often not a welcome visitor. Unfortunately the cruelty of some previous venturers had left an indelible impression upon the memory, making the European a suitable target for brutal murder.

An intrepid young Cambridge undergraduate, Ewart S Grogan, had, a few years previously, travelled through the region, exploring and studying the conditions of the inhabitants. He wrote in his journal,

> I asked him why all the people were so frightened, and where they had all gone: whereupon [he] proceeded to recount the same tales of misery and oppression that I'd heard the day before, from which I gathered that the Congo free state official, rejoicing in the name of Billy Gee, had suddenly swooped down on the country a year ago. After shooting down numbers of the [people], he had returned west carrying off fourteen young women, numerous children, all the cattle and goats, and putting a finishing touch to the proceedings, by a grand pyrotechnic display during which they bound the old women, threw them into the huts and then fired the roofs. Several absolutely independent witnesses informed me that this had been done actually in the presence of Billy Gee and the gentleman who accompanied him.

Such horrific tales of slaughter were not uncommon. It seems that certain colonisers and traders competed with the local inhabitants in barbarity.

Missionaries made much of cannibalism in their literature. It was a very evocative subject and described most graphically the depravity that gripped the African. By the time Studd entered the north-eastern district of the Congo the open practice of cannibalism had been brought under control by the Belgian officials in the areas where they had a presence. However, laws and rules don't change hearts, so what they actively discouraged took place out of sight. The Baleka tribe was particularly renowned for its savagery.

A lot of modern comment on the early missionaries' encounters with cannibalism brushes aside their reports as exaggerated talk. It has been said that such practices did not even exist but were the fruit of fertile imaginations to gain financial support. What follows is a traveller's account of the ravages of ferocious cannibal raids upon neighbouring peaceable agrarian tribes. These particular events occurred in the region of north-west Congo, west of Lake Albert, about the turn of the century. The account is reported in its full horror to answer those who would deny that such appalling practises happened.

As we travelled we were joined by numbers of Africans coming with loads of food. On enquiry I found they were refugees, having been driven out by the Baleka or Bareka, a tribe of cannibals from the Congo who had raided their country. Dead lined the paths showing that the tales of our companions were only too true. All the paths up the hills were lined with grain and torn skins, relics of those unfortunates who had been caught; and dried pools of blood, gaunt skeletons, grinning skulls, and trampled grass told a truly African tale. On arriving at the top of the ridge a beautiful rolling country opened out before us, dotted with clusters of grass huts and stately trees; russet patches of ripening mtama contrasted with the emerald green of the wild banana, range upon range of purple hills melted into the nether world of a tropical horizon. But we were not to enjoy the scenery long; we had been observed. The diabolical noise made by the onrushing tribesmen decided me that the matter was serious. I questioned my guide and was scarcely reassured by his naïve remark: "They are coming to eat us." I opened fire with my light rifle. We then hurried on to the huts from which we had seen these people come, but they fled. A cloud of vultures hovering over the spot gave me an inkling of what I was about to see, but the realisation defies description—it haunts my dreams. Loathsome, revolting, a hideous nightmare of horrors.

Every village had been burnt to the ground, and as I fled from the country I saw skeletons, skeletons everywhere and such postures. What tales of horror they told! Let this suffice: worse than all this I saw and that I have not exaggerated one jot or tittle, may God bear me witness . . . . I think it is advisable that those who have not the chance of seeing for themselves should know what is going on everyday in this country.

With such stories circulating, little wonder loved ones had tried to deter Studd and Buxton.

The hellish darkness which held the African captive only spurred Studd on. Fearless and refusing to count the cost, he marched to the battle and made it known he would continue alone if need be. One thing was certain: the devil had to be forced out of his entrenched position and the victory of Jesus established in the hearts of men.

They had left Mahagi without waiting for their personal luggage, which was to arrive jointly crated with that of the new AIM recruits. To remain there would possibly have been somewhat embarrassing since they were no longer part of the African Inland Mission. It seems Studd endeavoured to come to an agreement as to where he should locate. AIM decided on the more northern district so Buxton and Studd travelled south.

When they arrived at Kilo they were permitted to erect their tents in the compound of a local trader. Little did they know that they were to remain in these uncomfortable conditions for three months, waiting for their possessions and porters to carry the loads.

Delays are some of the most crucial experiences in a Christian's life. During such irksome periods motives are tested, desires refined and visions brought to clarity. It is also true that slack times can become virtual fiery furnaces, trying and testing every detail of the programme. Outwardly, waiting time appears to be wasted time, but spiritually an essential process is taking place. People, plans, projects and purposes tested in such fires prove they have the staying power to succeed. Almost every new venture passes through this experience, and fruitful servants of God would all testify to their own personal crucible of testing.

The principle of life out of death inexorably works. The plans for the death are tailor-made in heaven—we have no say in them. They are always unwelcome, causing problems and soul-searching. God has his own ways and means committee, and as someone has said, 'You are not included on it.' When the purpose is accomplished the trial ends, often as suddenly as it began. The Lord brings life out of death in a miraculous way, and the life continues, as long as the death is permanent.

The old campaigner Studd had walked this way before— but Alfred Buxton? He was about to learn something of the 'fellowship of his sufferings'—an introduction to a new depth of intimacy with his Lord. Don't let me give you the impression that C T was only an interested observer to this scene—that is not the case. Where the Spirit of the Lord is busy, lessons can be learnt. God's involvement in lives is never by accident, always by design. The future of C T Studd's final pioneer task was fought out in the heavenlies there in a tent behind a ramshackle store on the edge of the huge rain forest of Central Africa.

CHAPTER TWENTY-TWO

DARK KILO DAYS

DAY FOLLOWED DAY; nothing seemed to happen. The main street of Kilo was becoming too familiar. Studd, never one for standing still, grew impatient with the waiting.

The 'great gold mining centre' of Kilo consisted of one main road and African huts made of sticks with grass thatched roofs. The town's relative importance was marked by a resident Belgian government official. When Studd and Buxton first erected their tents in the Greek storekeeper's yard they never dreamt it would be weeks, then months, before their next move would be made. No doubt the powers of darkness had taken note that two indomitables had moved into their virgin territory, and certainly they would not allow their presence to go unchallenged.

Alfred Buxton, in his account of those 'dark' days at Kilo, registers their significance. So many trials and hopeless situations confined them that he likened their state to, 'Prisoners of the Lord, troubled on every side, perplexed, cast down but not destroyed.'

Before many days passed C T was stricken with fever. Young Buxton became nurse and doctor. With a mother's tenderness he cared for Studd when he seemed more dead than alive. Who can know what fearful thoughts went through that young man's mind? His only Christian fellowship was out of reach, lost in a fog of delirium. As good as alone in a very hostile land and without experience or language to communicate, it surely must have appeared that the fearful predictions of so many were to be fulfilled.

The indomitable spirit in Studd refused to lie down and die so easily; he revived and the fever passed—for a time. Weak but still fighting he began to busy himself with letters and plans for the future. If only the way would open up for them to move on to Dungu. Again and again hopes were raised with the promise of porters, who evaporated like mist just as regularly as they were expected.

Before Studd could dwell upon these things or have too much time to get impatient (he found the waiting intolerable) fever struck again. Already weak, the frail man was fighting for his life. When all seemed lost, amazingly he rallied only to succumb yet once more. He wrote later,

> That big ducking was an awkward affair, the fever mounted, the weakness increased, all medicines had failed and the time for disappearing seemed to have arrived; the darkest hour brought a brilliant flash of memory: "Is any sick let him call for the elders of the church and let them anoint him with oil, and the prayer of faith shall save the sick." Thank God for the saving sense of humour; there was but one 'elder' and he was in his twenty-second year; no matter, "one day is as a thousand years". But where was the oil? Neither salad, olive nor even linseed oil did we possess. What's the matter with lamp oil. The 'elder' brought in the lamp oil, dipped his finger, anointed my forehead then kneeled down and prayed. How God did it I don't know, nor do I care, but this I know that next morning whereas I was sick, nigh unto death, now I was healed.

He wrote home to Priscilla, 'The last go of fever was a very near thing but God had promised so plainly that even at the worst, I did not give up and I'm sure he will carry me right through and give us to serve him together for many years.' He had stared death in the face and rejoiced in Christ's victory. Undaunted he was ready to press on.

Alfred Buxton could truthfully describe their condition as troubled on every side. Whilst Studd had been fighting for his life, news came that Priscilla had collapsed—her heart condition had forced her into a semi-invalid existence.

In her need she wrote on her forty-ninth birthday, possibly unaware of the recurrent fevers that her husband had endured,

> I'm glad to say I'm now daily feeling a wee bit better, though my heart is not much to boast of. My own darling, how often I've longed and shall long for your return. How often I've longed to be with you, but I may not, dare not, dwell on all you must be suffering and enduring. I'm not strong enough to control myself and all emotion pulls me back, but I still hold to Psalm 34 and Daniel 3 that God will reunite us even down here.

Long weeks elapsed between their letters so that by the time Priscilla received her husbands's letter of August 9th she too was regaining her strength. He wrote, 'I'm getting better. Soon I will be able to do a good day's march; then I expect God will order the porters up.'

Neither Studd nor Buxton were familiar with the local, tropical climate. Photographs and books may mislead us into thinking that in such regions every sun-drenched day is followed by another one, equally hot and idyllic. The reality was far removed. Fierce tropical rain-storms, with winds strong enough to lift their tents and all their belongings way above the trees, swept down upon them. One tent was torn to shreds, and on many days they were drenched to the skin.

To add to their sense of being abandoned, disturbing letters kept arriving from home. The new committee was far from happy. The disruption with AIM had created violent ripples which now reached England. The situation was further aggravated by Studd's blunt accounts of the events as he saw them. The committee were talking of resigning. It seems there was barely a voice raised in his support.

Confrontational situations only sharpened Studd; he would never give in. The tougher the situation, the more he fought. Picking up his pen he lashed out. 'Tell the committee I'm not the man who has only gone to look and see, to pioneer and select stations; I've come to do the real job and fight for God against the devil.' So he responded to their 'treachery' in his usual fiery gusto, all guns blazing. He never knew how to use soft words. Repeatedly he likened his situation to General Gordon at Khartoum. Occasionally his loneliness echoed in a poignant note, only to be brusquely swept away in fighting words.

> The committee may all run like hares and rats if they please, I shall still stay and fight for Christ and the evangelisation of those unoccupied parts of the world; I fear nothing, neither men nor devils, neither death or hell. I am abiding with Jesus, and Jesus abides with me and that's plenty.

He wrote a careful letter to his son-in-law, Martin Sutton, who was one of the committee, but, in Studd fashion, he got so carried away with such strong talk that he sent the letter to his wife and asked her to interpret its contents, 'Gently, very gently as he feels I am too outspoken and blunt, and I would hurt his feelings.'

Everything Studd wrote during those perplexing days sounded a note of warfare. He was not a man to be conciliatory in the face of opposition; his response, almost as a reflex, was to defend and attack. Surprisingly his undaunted, courageous exterior hid a sensitive, easily hurt man. Actions which he interpreted to be disloyal caused him to smart painfully. He would not indulge in self-pity; rather he toughened himself and said to the effect, 'If they're chicken-hearted I'll go it alone!'

The committee's vacillation caused Studd such pain and frustration. He found himself completely unable to understand their misgivings or their behaviour. He said,

> It is well to look things right in the eye and for God to try us like Gideon. When he has tried us to the utmost we shall come forth like gold. I really believe God has got us in tow and that he intends to execute his work of evangelising the world. By God's grace I intend to be in the job for all I'm worth come life or come death, committee or no committee, helper or no helper.

In contrast to this abrasive side of Studd's character he took time in the midst of troubles and sickness to order from England a special New Testament with notes and cross references as a present for Alfred. On another occasion he obtained a processing kit for his photography. Behind the stubborn, prickly front there was a very feeling, loving man. He constantly asked after all the members of the family and sent most tender greetings to his mother who wrote regularly to him. During the difficulties at Kilo he was to become a grandfather. Dorothy had her first child.

Priscilla had been busy since her husband's departure. Despite her poor health she remained remarkably buoyant in spirit, supporting her husband's venture, ignoring the opposition and doubts even among their own family and close friends on the committee. She produced a magazine advertising the new Heart of Africa Mission. Studd praised her achievement but had one reservation: 'You put so many photos of me in it that I am ashamed to send it to anyone, and I so fear others calling it "Studd's mission".'

On another occasion he expressed his reluctance at being called 'the leader' of the mission. This seemed to be a reaction to the structure of other missionary societies; he did not want the HAM to be formed in their mould. He said, 'Jesus is our leader and each one is to follow him.' Despite this attitude, his own leadership was so clear and unchallenged that of course every volunteer who joined him recognised it or left. Idealistically he only looked for missionaries with pioneer qualities like his own, expecting each one to have their own calling, faith and vision.

Once C T's health began to improve life settled down to something of a routine. On the 9th of August he wrote,

> Our days are spent thus,-
> Rise as soon as light, soon after 5.00am.
> Have a cup of tea.
> Read Bible separately till breakfast at 8.00.
> Work 9–1.
> Then after lunch read and pray together.
> Then Alf reads to me sometimes for a while; the fever has knocked me about.
> Then work again till after 5.00pm when we go for a stroll.
> Return, have supper and go to bed about 9.00pm.

Studd was renowned for his incredible appetite for work. Daylight was never squandered by sleeping. Regardless of the negative reports he was receiving from home, the territorial claims of various missions and his present, seemingly futile wait at Kilo, he busied himself writing and preparing a number of little booklets. One, called *Christ's Etceteras,* was an expansion of the five principles, or 'five smooth stones' as he called them, that he had outlined eighteen months previously. This unusual little document became the foundation for the aims and principles of the mission. Constantly the evangelisation of the whole world occupied his thoughts, and its recurring theme is mentioned thirty-eight times in the sixteen page booklet. Marooned in a tent at Kilo, miles from anywhere, Studd wrote, 'The object of the new mission is the speediest possible fulfilment of the command of Christ to evangelise the whole world, by a definite attempt to evangelise the remaining unevangelised parts of the earth.' He even wrote to his old friend from China days, Stanley P Smith, suggesting he should take on the task of enlisting and training recruits for Asia.

Charles fed deeply from the word of God, and during those days he was wonderfully blessed by reading John's Gospel. It seemed to shout aloud to him, 'Do you now believe?' He said,

> Christ's rules of discipleship are so plain and forcible, there is no getting over the fact that he meant his disciples to stop at nothing, but make sacrifices similar to his own. Yet does anyone do such a thing? More than half the Christians would shout, "fanatic" or, "crazy-head".

Alfred Buxton used his days trying to learn the rudiments of Bangala, the local trade language. At the same time his peaceable nature was being educated in Studd's school of spiritual warfare. Outwardly their position was pathetic, but spiritually Studd knew the battle in the heavenlies was joined. War waged about them while they remained captive, prisoners of the Lord. Victory would be theirs—an open door into the unevangelised districts or Central Africa.

God chose the right man, one prepared to be called 'mad' and a 'fool'—but he was in good company. Lord Wolseley said, 'A soldier, like a missionary, to be of any use must be a fanatic.' Studd commented, 'Absolutely true! I hate this sickly, lollipoppy religion of today—may God uproot it and give us the real genuine article!'

The Bible says, '. . . the whole world is under the control of the evil one' (1 Jn 5:19, NIV). When Studd entered the Congo Satan ruled undisturbed in his domain. He had hardly been challenged—the strong man was keeping his goods. It is pointless for any Christian worker to think they can walk into such territory and immediately see conversions. The Bible explains how to be effective: '... how can anyone enter a strong man's house and carry off his possessions unless he first ties up the strong man? Then he can rob his house' (Mt 12:29, NIV). Revelation 12:10 tells us how Satan is overcome: '... they loved not their lives unto the death' (Rev 12:10).

Already Studd had said that going to Africa cost him his life; in other words, it cost him everything. He was in a sense a martyr laying down his life for the people of the Congo.

His determined resolve to die to self and serve God almost became a fact during the dark days at Kilo. It seems as if Satan was allowed to try him almost to the point of death, but through it all Studd's obedience didn't even flicker. He refused to be diverted from the heavenly call. 'If it means death—I'd rather die than go back.' Satan has no ammunition against such an indomitable attitude, full of faith and obedience. When a man is dead there is nothing Satan can do except yield up the ground—the captives must go free.

The intolerable inconvenience, the sickness, the bad news from home, being forsaken by friends and associates, the spoilt relationships with other missions, the loneliness, the fear of being abandoned, the embarrassment of being 'unofficial', the feeling of futility and failure, the fierce storms and lack of basic comforts—all of these added together turned up the heat under the crucible of the lives of Studd and Buxton.

The frontier between the kingdom of God and the kingdom of darkness is marked by the cross. Studd lifted it high, proclaiming its victory as he yielded and died. His faith cried out victoriously and the demons had to flee. The power of the strong man was broken—two weak men, one as good as dead, were coming to rob him of his goods.

An incredible spiritual battle was waged in that tent, and the victory gained is according to a principle that never changes. A corn of wheat fell into the ground and died and so produced much fruit.

June, July and August were nearly past. For three months these two front-line soldiers had battled and now it was the devil who had to retreat and let them past. On the 28th of August, 1913, seventy-three porters were gathered. Thankfully Alfred Buxton and Charles Studd collapsed their tents and began the final stage of their journey. Repeatedly CT had said he intended making Dungu his base, but, as he was to discover, further disappointments awaited him.

CHAPTER TWENTY-THREE

THE HEART OF AFRICA

THE SQUABBLES, noise and arguments continued till the last load was picked up and the line of porters wended their way out of the village in the first light of dawn, heading for Dungu. Each man's prime interest was to carry the smallest, lightest load, so every morning was marred by ugly scenes whilst they verbally battled it out before setting off.

C T and Buxton eventually left Kilo at 12.30 midday on the 28th of August, 1913. Their path led through forest which clad the sides of hills laying in ridges for hundreds of miles. No roads, motor vehicles, or even animals would assist them on their journey. They had to walk or, where possible, cycle.

The gently undulating terrain was all above 3,000 feet. Daily it revealed its delights to Studd who was fascinated by the vast variety of trees, plants, insects and wild life. Fortunately his strength had returned and he was able to walk and negotiate the surprising obstacles that lay before them. Some days the two men endured torrential rain which made the paths deep in mud and swelled the rivers. For eleven days their route lay through the vast, dense Ituri forest where the

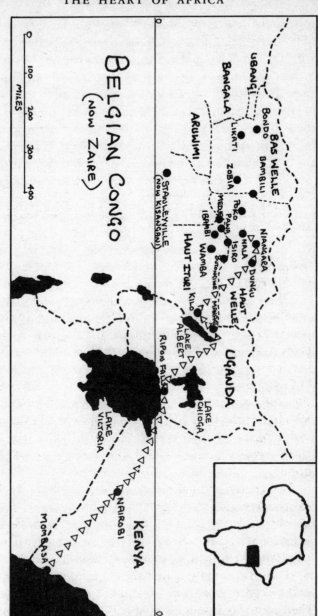

The area of Africa where HAM worked, showing the route taken by
Charles Studd and Alfred Buxton

sun barely penetrated. Bogs, fallen trees, huge exposed tree roots and dense undergrowth, defied the use of their cycles, so with the aid of stout sticks they clambered up and down the hills of red earth, which were as slippery as if they had been soaped. It became an achievement to remain upright. They pushed their bicycles up steep rocky paths and down again, then bumped across broken stone slabs, not good for the bikes, but as Studd said, 'Good for the liver!' When defeated, the bikes were carried on porters' heads and they walked.

The whole route was like a giant obstacle race with every kind of device to hinder. But Charles Studd barely gave the conditions of travel a thought; he was overjoyed to be on the move. Luxuries and comfort in life were of so little importance to him that one could have labelled him as ascetic. If rats ran round his bed at night he would make a joke of it. If he was drenched to the skin he would enjoy changing his clothes— but never grumble. If he only had porridge to eat three times a day he would say, 'The food is delicious,' and be thankful. Always he made light of hardships, and always he was able to see the funny side of any situation. His asceticism was that of one who was dead to the need of comfort and luxury for the sake of Christ.

Leaving Kilo seemed suddenly to bring their final objective into sight. Soon they would reach Dungu. Anticipating their arrival lightened their spirits, but it was not to last—after only four days they were again halted. The porters would go no further. Studd waited impatiently for fifteen days while others were induced or cajoled into working. He said, 'Delays are the greatest trial to me.' The local people were never too keen to work as they could live adequately from their fields and the forest—they had no pressing need for extra finance.

On the 17th September they walked out of the Semmé Poste with a new band of carriers and went on to Arebi, a military Poste, stopping overnight at villages on the way. The Belgian government exercised its colonial rule over the

Congo by having its officials stationed all over the country, resident at 'The Poste'. C T was always very sociable, wherever he went he made a point of meeting the local officials. From them he learned about the local tribes and with their assistance arranged porters and food supplies.

He enjoyed the adventure of seeing new places, and at times he must have looked like a strange foreign tourist draped about with cameras. He was a keen photographer, recording many surprising and beautiful scenes.

Accompanying some photographs he sent home, he wrote,

> ... Alimasie is very beautiful, lovely, a veritable paradise. Mountains surround us with outcrops of rock and everywhere giant trees and palms complete the scene. Nestling beneath them are little huts with dried grass roofs. I slept on the veranda at night with a revolver by my side—the place abounds in leopards.

Wildlife was abundant and was enjoyed whilst it kept a reasonable distance! The brilliant fluorescent green mamba, an exceptionally dangerous snake, found its way into their tents, but God delivered them.

While repairing the third puncture of the day C T couldn't resist photographing the local beauties. The women were 'made up' Congo style, with intricate designs of stripes and dots painted on their faces and bodies in a black dye. Their hair arrangements were quite amazing. The thick fuzzy mat of hair was plaited into dozens of short, fine plaits which were arranged into a multitude of varying designs. Some even had them sticking out in spikes all over their heads.

The path to Dungu was at times smooth, when they made good use of their bicycles, but more often it was like crossing railway lines as they bumped their way over the network of tree roots and rocks. As they pedalled along, singing at the tops of their voices, they would be on the lookout for any suitable addition to their menu. Both the guinea fowl and the

African pheasant, with its fantastic plumage, made a choice meal. There was never any need to go hungry. Studd wrote, 'This is a land of plenty: rice, millet, monkey nuts, bananas, sweet potatoes and pineapples abound in a well-cultivated haven.' In that tropical region everything grew seemingly effortlessly and almost visibly.

When Studd and Buxton entered the Congo it was agreed with the AIM that they would open a station at Dungu, leaving Faradje in the North to AIM. Studd understood that to be the agreement and made all his plans in accordance. Dungu was to be their first station. He even wove the name into a little jingle which he sang as a proclamation of his faith. He considered it to be eminently suited, especially as no other missions were in the vicinity.

It was a relief to leave the dripping Ituri forest behind; they had had enough of its depressing gloom. Out in the bright

C T Studd playing his banjo

sunshine they cycled with happy hearts through the beautiful grassland of the Wellé province. The elephant grass stood so high that at times their path seemed like a narrow corridor between ten to twelve foot high walls which opened out into a fruitful, peaceful land. They reached Dungu on the 8th of October, 1913, six weeks after leaving Kilo.

Immediately they made for the post office—such as it was—and there they received some devastating news. The local official welcomed them, handed over their mail and then added, 'You will not be alone here; four other missionaries are resident now.' He recited their names, 'Morris, Batstone, Miller and Clarke.' Dumbfounded and very angry, Studd took the mail and left. So Morris and Batstone of the AIM had gone ahead of them and located at Dungu after agreeing to leave it to Studd! The Greek storekeeper told them that the new missionaries had only been there ten days and had already applied for land to establish a mission.

A certain Mr Moffatt kindly assisted the affronted Studd and bewildered Buxton with a good dinner and a bath, but C T could not rest. As soon as it was possible he went to visit Morris and Batstone; Miller and Clarke were unknown to him. He wanted to get the story straight fron the 'horse's mouth' and to tell them just what he thought about their behaviour!

He learned that after agreeing to go to Faradje they had changed their minds as another mission was well established there. Studd considered their whole argument thin because the only other mission was Roman Catholic and its presence was well-known. In his own blunt, attacking way he told them exactly what he thought: 'I let out all my feelings. I gave it to him straight and direct.' To find that the launching ground for their endeavour was taken from under their noses made Studd so angry he couldn't sleep at night. It was an incredible disappointment after months of planning and battling against endless opposition. It seemed to Studd that the powers of darkness were determined to prevent them opening up the land.

Alfred Buxton, a gentle, conciliatory character, tried to bring some healing to the situation, and Batstone too made every effort to mend the breach—but Studd would have none of it. For an Englishman, a university man, a gentleman and a Christian, to act so dishonourably was, in Studd's eyes, dastardly. His own view of the situation was so heavily coloured by his extreme sense of honour that he could not receive anything they said. Alfred tried to gently chide Studd about his unchristian speech which only provoked a sharper reaction. C T thought,

> Alf is desperately weak about such things, fearing the face of man. He is such a mixture, so loveable, loving and generous, self-denying in the extreme, but desperately weak in the battle. Alf is always seeking to stand well with everybody. I would like to see some fire in him, but he suffers with the fear of man. I say to Alf, It's no use squinting around to see what folk think, or what will be the result of actions or words. The only way is to look at the thing, know the right, and do and say it at all costs whatever happens.

Alfred came through this trouble the tougher, but we can see how Studd's warring character confused the issue.

Whenever C T Studd waded into battles of this sort he was convinced that he was upholding truth and honour. Any failure to do what had been said and any speech that he considered subtle and deceptive had to be openly confronted. He considered this his Christian duty, so as to reveal sin and discharge his responsibility to his brother in Christ.

In the middle of all the sharp contention Studd learned that Clarke was seriously sick with fever, so he walked over to his house to visit him. Although his words were sharp and warring whenever he felt the honour of Christ was at stake he could be just as quick in forgiveness and generous with gifts and money, even to those who had wronged him.

When it was evident that the AIM was firmly established at Dungu he meekly said, 'I shall now proceed further west and open Niangara, God willing. Surely it was Niangara that the great explorer and scientist Dr Schweinfurth in the 1870s described as the "very heart of Africa".' This appealed to Studd.

In the heat of all their difficulties C T Studd barely had time to consider his news from home. Priscilla was still unwell. All he could do was pray for her and hope for better news. He wrote her a concerned letter, but was mercifully unaware of the seriousness of her condition. He added, 'I'm fit, I have only had a small touch of dysentry and my chest is good.' Asthma was still a trial.

At the end of an emotionally exhausting day they retired to their house to pray. The heavens were black with heavy clouds, then, in an instant, the rain fell in sheets. Incredible

C T Studd at work in the Congo

claps of thunder interrupted their prayers, and a deafening crack sounded right overhead. The light went out and plaster fell down upon them. Sitting shocked in the inky darkness they realised that lightning had struck their house. Rushing outside, they stood in the drenching rain where excitable voices competed with the din of the torrent. A wisp of smoke rose from the grass thatching, but in their ignorance they considered the sheeting rain would thoroughly douse the fire.

Soaked to the skin they retreated inside, but a crowd had gathered shouting and yelling, telling them to get their belongings out and to run from the fire. Suddenly there was no time to lose; in energetic panic they shoved their kit outside into the torrential rain, returning again and again till everything was rescued. The fire took hold deep in the grass roof and in a flash engulfed everything. The flames won over the torrents of water. As a crowning celebration, an abandoned box of cartridges gave a cracker display!

An important Belgian official, Count de Grunne, had already shown Alfred Buxton and Charles Studd warm hospitality. When the news of the fire reached him he ran with only a towel tied about him to see what assistance he could give. He soon took control of the situation and, as if he was ordering an item on a menu, sent a man to make another house ready for the visitors. 'His kindness was so great that he was like an angel to us.'

A few days later new porters were engaged and the beleaguered friends moved on. The time spent at Dungu had been valuable, if only because of the beautiful friendship that was forged between C T Studd and Count de Grunne. He supplied them with so much useful information, and during the period of obtaining land concessions his help was invaluable. They learned that Dungu was to be evacuated by the government and Niangara would take its place. As a result Dungu would wane in importance and Niangara would grow.

It was heartening to learn that Bangala, the language that

Alfred had already begun to master, was the language of the villages along the main roads and, with French, was understood at the government postes.

Some pleasant days were to follow whilst they were taken down the Wellé river in canoes paddled by standing men. They turned a bend in the river and the tempo of life changed abruptly—now they were shooting down rapids. None of them fancied being thrown into the water, the haunt of crocodiles and hippopotami.

Mighty trees festooned with creepers obliterated the view beyond the river-banks, which were thick with matted undergrowth. Bird sounds constantly filled the air, although the little creatures eluded the trained binoculars. From time to time a small village in a clearing would come into view where swarms of brilliant butterflies danced on the beach along the water's edge. The scene looked idyllic, but that illusion soon evaporated as the biting river flies made their presence felt. Unfortunately their bites caused more than annoyance; a young missionary some years later died when she succumbed to the fever and septic skin condition their poisonous bites produced.

With days to contemplate their arrival C T wondered if 'Niangara had already been snapped up.' What would he find when he arrived? He was aware that the Roman Catholics had occupied all the principal places. They had received large land concessions from the Belgian government. Every assistance was afforded them, whereas Protestant missions had no such friends—even government policy discriminated against them.

The people in the riverside villages were unhelpful and preferred to ignore the white man and his demands for food, shelter and carriers. Exasperated by one chief man's lack of respect and willingness, Studd took matters into his own hands. Like any colonial of his day he threatened the men with a revolver and soon got what he wanted! Out of the fast-fading light men came running and gave him every assistance. The usual colonial method of exacting village hospitality was to lock the chief man up in a hut, guarded by an armed man, until he guaranteed compliance!

On the 16th October, 1913, the canoes were pulled up on to the beach at Niangara. With incredible relief their loads were dumped at the landing point. They stretched their legs and took their first look around.

CHAPTER TWENTY-FOUR

ESTABLISHING
A BRIDGEHEAD

BARELY HAD THEIR canoes beached at Niangara before Studd, anxious to know the potential of the district, was planning an investigation tour. He said, 'We are the farthest outpost of God's work; there is nothing west, north or south of us, till you strike the Congo river.' What he said was perfectly true. South of the Congo river, the Baptist Missionary Society had established an extensive flourishing work; but north of the river for hundreds and hundreds of miles, there was not one Protestant missionary.

For two months the travellers were given the luxury of a house by a kind official. The thick grass thatching kept them cool—such a contrast to their tents. Everything was pleasing; it seemed the Lord had perfectly directed their paths. They praised and thanked God; he had caused them to triumph over every satanic device designed to keep them out of the land.

A few days were taken to reassess their position, then the mail arrived: a jumble of letters revealing a troubled mosaic of happenings in England. Anxiously Studd read of Priscilla's illness—she had almost died—and then thankfully of her slight improvement. She had been struck down again with her heart condition and like an invalid was unable to leave her bed. Charlie read on and learned that Lord Radstock, a faithful friend, had visited Priscilla and prayed for her. Immediately she experienced a remarkable measure of healing. Because of the capricious mail delivery, Charlie had learned the good news before he knew the fearful extent of her very dangerous condition. The doctor sent a detailed account, intended to impress upon Charles the necessity of his return. How he thanked God for the order in which he received his mail! 'The Lord was not only a wonderful Counsellor, but also a wonderful postmaster!'

Overflowing with gratitude, he thanked all who had so lovingly tended Priscilla in her time of need. He struggled as he wrote, hating to leave her alone; yet resolutely he mustered his will and said, 'It's best I do not return at this time. First of all I must obey Christ, and I will trust you to his hands.'

C T had hardly recovered from the trauma of Priscilla's sickness, when in December, 1913, in one delivery of mail he had news of the death of Lord Radstock and Martin Sutton, his son-in-law, the husband of Grace, his eldest daughter. Both had died within the same week. The loss of these two gallant supporters—Lord Radstock, a long-standing friend and referee for the committee, and Martin, the chairman— almost brought a final death blow to the home end of the work. Priscilla, in her frail state, virtually carried on single-handed.

Studd's first impressions of Niangara were most favourable. The people were pleasant, the location good, and very soon a sizeable land allocation was negotiated with the help of Count de Grunne. They discovered that they were in the centre of a group of tribes: the Bazande, Mangbetu, Medje, Nepoko, the Pygmies, and many others. What an opportunity! Almost beyond their wildest dreams.

The two men rejoiced—the efforts of the past nine months

were rewarded with a fine location for the mission's head-quarters, surely the seal of God upon their faith. By April they moved into their own permanent house.

A strenuous journey was made to Nala—a five day walk—where they were delighted to find a place ever more pleasing. Nala, an abandoned government post, had some brick-built houses, a wide open parade ground, and a gracious avenue of palms. Living conditions would pose no problem. Everywhere had an abundance of food and water and few mosquitoes. The two men were elated; their dreams of evangelising the whole district now came within the bounds of possibility. Studd wrote to the committee. 'We will need a doctor and a teacher for Nala. Send us good recruits, we need *men*. Where will the funds come from? They will come from God. Nala is a magnificent station, a golden opportunity.' One has to love Studd—he was an incredible enthusiast. He bubbled with anticipation. In the eye of faith he saw Nala a busy, func-

The congregation—every man brought his own deckchair

tioning mission station, with school and hospital.

Further tours made in different directions yielded a harvest of hopes for the future. They discovered people—plenty of them—and everywhere they received a warm welcome. The promise of more land concessions confirmed they were in the will of God.

By the end of 1914 Studd had secured land concessions at four places: Niangara, Nala, Poko and Bambili. The possibility of others was always dangling before him like the proverbial carrot. As he toured, the vision of dozens of new works drove him to write desperate and, at times, scathing letters home. If only he could get volunteers to take up the task! When he asked the Belgian officials for concessions, he was greeted, to his surprise, with openness. 'Oh! Yes certainly, what is it you want?' Then followed the repeated question, 'But how many men do you have to man these stations?'

While the door swung wide open in the Congo and he saw encouragement on every hand, Studd, battle-worn got caught unawares by a ferocious attack on the home front. The consequences of his separation from the AIM rumbled on, and in England it caused many people to be disaffected from Studd's cause. Few could be persuaded to volunteer. Priscilla wrote that his name had become a public scandal.

The enemy subtly marshalled his forces, and Studd unwittingly failed to see his tactics. It seems Charles Studd knew no different way of dealing with disagreements other than strongly defending himself to every interested party and, in the process, spreading the problem. His 'straight talk' and warring accusations isolated him and the work of the HAM. Priscilla chided him for writing such hard censorious letters and upsetting those near and dear to him. But he was in no mood to hear even her gentle rebuke, and, in defensive stance, he hit back equally hard at her. 'I have to be straight, I'm required by God to be—if I do not warn him, his blood would be on my head.'

The peaceable Alfred could do little to influence Studd when he became locked into a warring attitude. C T said, 'Alf will make a warrior yet!' What a school! What was Alfred to say when Studd defended himself saying, 'Do not give him a spoonful of treacle when he requires a downright good pummelling, so as to make him repent and get right with God!'

Priscilla remained incredibly loyal to her husband during this vexing period, although she could see the folly of some of his reactions. Being confined to her bed for the best part of the day did not hinder her from very actively promoting the work. She organised prayer meetings, produced a magazine, and on a dozen fronts pushed forward the claims of the unevangelised world.

In the Congo opportunity blossomed, but at the home end there seemed to be nothing but difficulties. Priscilla, somewhat better now that the acute stage of her sickness had passed, still existed as a chronically ill person, only able to be up half a day. Financially the work looked hopeless, support had dwindled, and controversy raged over a financial policy. In essence there were those on the home committee totally committed to trusting God and not making their needs known, but others, now faced with a dire situation, were ready to change that policy. Studd, a man of implicit, childlike faith, could not tolerate this vacillating. He had decided to trust God, and circumstances were never going to change that. He wrote, 'Our trust is in God, not in man or common sense. Müller was tested, can we expect anything different?' His broad shoulders of faith carried them, rather than the committee supporting him. He wrote them a loving letter to encourage their faith.

Tucked away in the heart of Africa, at the end of a very uncertain line of communication, he became extremely frustrated. He longed for men and women who would trust God in simplicity; he only wanted a committee who would echo his own heart convictions.

The commission to evangelise those areas without the gospel weighed so heavily upon Studd's heart that all his waking hours were devoted to strategising to see the task accomplished. The lack of recruits bitterly disappointed him. Plans were laid and opportunities abounded, but where were the men? He was looking for a rare breed: those with the same heart as his own, prepared to go out to anything or nothing and who would trust God, not the society, for their every need. Women volunteered, but he could not receive them till a married couple were first installed.

He began to plan a visit home to gather a new band of missionaries. For some time he dithered about Alfred also returning so that he could marry Edith — but Alfred finally convinced Studd that he should stay.

Alfred's decision to remain was very costly. Edith wrote frequently and appealed to her father to assist them to be married quickly. With great wisdom, tact and love, he advised his daughter, encouraging her to trust God and prepare with adequate training for the future. Gently he warned her of the need to sacrifice and defer their marriage till God made a way. He said, 'I may not kiss and fondle as much as others . . . but I love you.' Tenderly he helped her to accept Alfred's decision.

The political scene darkened, and the dread news broke that Britain was at war with Germany. Great uncertainty hit the church; would men leave their country for mission work when patriotism demanded they volunteer to fight for their king and country? Charles Studd was in no doubt where the Christian's first loyalty lay; had he battled this far, now to be left holding the fort alone?

While such dismal news continued to arrive from home, the two men enjoyed exploring the area by cycle or, when conditions dictated, on foot. At times these journeys drew out from Studd his last resources of energy. Sick, hot, dirty, hungry and exhausted, he would arrive at a village where only the rowdy welcome would revive him. The children, full of fun, tore along beside their cycles shouting and yelling. The women joined in—never had they seen such a sight before. The day ended with Alfred giving cycle rides to the chief!

Studd was not an idle sightseer. He carefully documented every place visited, for its suitability as a station, availability of supplies and, most important of all, the density of its population.

The need for Studd to return home became increasingly apparent. A new committee had been appointed. Priscilla had done an amazing job locating those willing to serve and who were people of faith. But Studd's presence was necessary; he remained the director of the work and in those early days was its architect, even in detail.

Priscilla celebrated her fiftieth birthday. Charles wrote a tender, most appreciative letter for all she had accomplished since he had left. He recognised her amazing achievements in the face of fantastic opposition. He knew, without a doubt, that she was bound to him in vision and determination to see the work proceed and Jesus glorified.

He said, 'The Lord has set us in the ring to fight the devil to the last. He has greatly honoured us as a family.' He likened Priscilla and himself to two batsmen in a game of cricket, she on the home end, keeping the innings going.

A cable arrived with the heartening news of recruits on the way. C T decided that the time had now come for him to go home. Alfred would not be left alone, and the work could progress. Alfred had completed another Bangala vocabulary and was well equipped to help the newcomers with language and orientation.

Sadly, before the group were to step foot on Congo soil, one of their number, Mr Bowers, died of typhoid. This soberly underlined the fact that they were engaged in a vicious spiritual war. Before Studd had recovered from the shock, news arrived of another death: Count de Grunne, who had been a most valuable friend and aid to the work, had succumbed to fever.

Charles Studd went home to announce, 'Our opportunities are expanding each day, the more we know the more there is to do. The land is open before us. Where are the recruits? We need spiritual men, then women, to come and occupy the places of opportunity.' He was not concerned whether they were ordained or highly educated. He said, 'Why seek higher education when what we need is a bricklayer who will talk of Christ — he doesn't need theology.'

The Heart of Africa Mission had become, by its availability, a tool in the hand of God.

CHAPTER TWENTY-FIVE

ONE HANDFUL OF BLESSING MIXED WITH TWO OF TRIAL

THE PARTING WITH Alfred Buxton was hard. In a farewell letter, Studd wrote, 'He has given me you, my precious Alf, how can I do ought but praise him.' This most unlikely couple had been joined together by their united baptism into trial and suffering. Their love sprang from the deep roots of a shared passion for the lost. 'We marvelled at what God had accomplished in spite of us, one being too old and the other too young; he uses whomever he will and chiefly likes the fools, the weak, and the nobodies.'

Journeying to the west coast, Studd systematically gathered travel details, even the steamer timings on the River Congo, to aid future parties. His thoughts were always two jumps ahead, planning for all contingencies.

Studd sailed home to war-weary Britain in early 1915. An unrealistic optimism carried him along; surely it would be over soon. He said, 'The war is just one more trial of faith, but we laugh at the idea of its hindering us.' Sadly the 1914–1918 war became a major interruption in the advance of the gospel for all missionary societies.

Number 17 Highland Road always seemed to be bulging

with people — mainly women — including a number of prospective missionaries. Charles found it somewhat irritating to be perpetually competing with so many others for a little time with his wife. As soon as possible, he left to tour the country — preaching and stirring up the lethargic church. The Home Committee had a shake-up, and he injected a new fiery tone into the magazine.

To the committee, Studd must have seemed like a hopeless dreamer. He insisted that the vision for the mission be nothing less than the whole unevangelised world. The Heart of Africa Mission was only its beginning. His eyes were already scanning every needy field, where he expected others to take up the responsibility. Patiently the committee members remonstrated with him. They knew the facts. There was barely enough money to accomplish the present task without looking farther afield. Studd refused to budge; he had heard God. When he wrote to Alfred he said, 'Worldwide it is! Thank God I don't know how to retreat!' Studd's visit finally secured the faith policy of the mission. He had gathered a group of people who were prepared to believe for impossibilities with him.

Charles promised Edith to take her to the Congo as soon as possible, but delay followed delay. Recruits were ready to sail, but there were no funds to send them. Financial restraints almost strangled the work and unconsciously moulded its spartan style.

Despite the austerity measures Studd demanded, the work in the Congo villages continued to bear fruit. The first three baptisms had taken place at Nala in 1915, then news came from Alfred of more and more turning to Christ. The shortage of money put Studd in a tension. He chided: 'Away with fancy plans and any extravagance — we will not take our example from other missions, only from God and the Scriptures.' He saw every pound spent on non-essentials as a pound less to open up a new station. He became quite fanatical about it, even complaining that some missionaries ate too much!

In the meantime Alfred, although still only twenty-three years old, carried the full responsibility for the work. Studd urged him to remember their objective—evangelism. Alfred hardly needed that exhortation. He toured the stations, encouraging the new missionaries and helping them with language and orientation, as well as caring for the young churches. He continued translating Mark's Gospel into Bangala and prepared a vocabulary and grammar for printing. Above all, he endeared himself to all who knew him by his gentle, loving nature.

The war scene at home made Studd gloomy—he felt sure it signalled the end of the world. His articles and preaching constantly echoed the war theme. 'Where are the soldiers for Christ? Where are those prepared to fight the devil?' So often he left people wondering if his manner of speech and writing was really Christian. He was accused of flippancy—of being amusing rather than spiritual, and at times, cuttingly cruel, as he lashed at half-hearted Christians with his words. He made his point in a unique style. 'The light of sacrifice makes every place a chamber of horrors to the devil and sends him flying to hell with dark glasses!' He prodded people with a poignant story.

> A talented man said, "God has so plainly commanded me to go at once to Central Africa, that I could never again believe in the Bible if I don't obey." Yet he didn't obey. An old prophet turned him aside. His excuse? A varicose vein! (Loud laughter—in hell).

Articles written in like manner appeared in the Heart of Africa magazine. Some hated them, and said so; others praised his forthrightness.

In Charles Studd's mind, the question of whether he should return to the Congo never arose; he could not imagine anything else. The decision had been made before he came home, and nothing would change it. His health during this period had not been good—fever struck him down many times—but he took it all in his stride. He certainly did not intend asking any doctors for their opinion, but preferred, as always, to do his own home doctoring.

Eventually a party of eight were gathered, including Edith. Pauline watched; she too would later follow them. As the farewells were made there loomed something almost tragic in the pained family group. Edith—fearful and uncertain; going to marry a man she hadn't seen for almost four years and becoming a 'reluctant missionary'. Then her father—fifty-six years old, with steel-like resolution, returning to the land of his calling, never to put his foot again on English soil. And Priscilla—outwardly so tough, but inwardly crying; outwardly sending, but inwardly clinging. She was thankfully unaware of the trials that lay ahead.

During the voyage C T called his troops together each day and utilised every waking moment to equip them for the rigours they would encounter. Hours passed, spent either studying the language or the great heroes of faith. During this phase of the mission's history, those volunteering for the field came untrained and ill-prepared for the spiritual hostility and their primitive living conditions.

Their boat entered the mouth of the River Congo on the 27th of September, 1916. Thankfully, Studd pulled himself on deck—he had been sick for fifteen days. Alfred came to meet the party, and Edith—once she had spoken to her man on the bottom deck of the river boat, among the goats and chickens—knew it was going to be all right. When they left the river there remained a month's trekking ahead of them, then Nala.

What a reception! Before they approached the village a forward party came out to welcome them. Unfettered exuberance spilled over—Studd was back. Accompanied by music,

C T Studd in 1916 ready to go again

drums, shouting and singing, the cavalcade entered the village and then endless handshaking and back-slapping followed. The new believers pressed to be introduced, and Studd rejoiced in his heart at the quality of the converts. Nala now boasted sixty baptised, but the crowd that day was swelled with intrigued onlookers.

Alfred's carefully laid plans went off perfectly. Studd couldn't help being most impressed, and by the obvious progress he saw. The jungle had been cut, excellent houses built for the newcomers, and even a house boy had been trained for each one so as to ease their transition into Congo-style living. Village life could be a shock, without privacy, furniture, sanitation, running water and many basic western foods.

Three weeks later, the first white wedding in Central Africa took place. C T Studd had the privilege of marrying Edith and Alfred at Niangara, followed by the civil affair, conducted in French, by the local Belgian official. Everybody looked so smart in their resurrected suits, they hardly recognised each other!

A mixed picture of the work unfolded as Studd took charge again. In virgin territory new converts abounded, with many baptisms. The chiefs were now requesting missionaries to come. In dozens of places, land and buildings had been offered if they would open a school and teach them about God. A wide open door stood before them. God even sealed the work with signs and miracles.

A dead man, while being laid in his grave, came back to life and told of seeing a vision of white men coming with words of life. He was told, 'Wait for the man who will tell you how to escape the flames.'

The new converts were instructed to spread the gospel and became the most efficient evangelists. Soon the churches were sending them out two by two and training some as preachers. A ripe harvest was being reaped. How the missionaries praised God as they looked into the happy faces of these new Christians! They knew what a victory the blood of Jesus had accomplished in their lives.

In the established stations, the story was not the same; there they had met resistance. Enthusiasm had dimmed and the Christians found it hard to walk in the Spirit—not surprising when one looked at the darkness all around. The normal life of the African defied imagination. The chiefs ruled their tribes in a strict feudal system controlled by fear and cruelty. Polygamy was the norm, with one notable chief having 2,000 wives! These poor creatures were nothing but slaves, often brutally treated. The women did all the work, preparing fields, growing and collecting food, cooking and carrying water, besides bearing the babies.

Sin was their only pastime. Public opinion upheld immorality, approving and accepting sinful relationships as normal. The warp and woof of society defied description with bestial acts, depraved behaviour, lust and licentiousness, initiated in witchcraft. Life in the villages was ruled by hellish spirits. The faces of innocent children soon became clouded with the vile expressions of cruelty, murder and devilry, which characterised those of older age.

Jesus demonstrated to these hopelessly lost people that he was able to save to the uttermost. The shining faces of the new converts gave ample evidence of the truth of his promises.

Studd took up residence in Nala and saw a steady growth in the church. As the years passed hundreds believed. Then sadly, stories of backsliding and sin came to light. Many who had been baptised turned again to their immorality and witchcraft—even leaders in the church. C T was broken-hearted. He preached and pleaded for repentance, but hearts were hard. Now he prayed for the fear of the Lord and a deep work of the Spirit to bring conviction of sin. Studd, whose judgements were only black or white and who knew nothing of the vagueness in between, could no longer accept the backsliders as believers. He quoted 1 John 3:8: 'He who does what is sinful is of the devil. . .' (NIV). Determined to cleanse the church, the sinners were called to account, questioned, judged and put out of the church. Unfortunately their new life in Christ had only scratched the surface of the granite-like heathenism of so many.

An inquest was held to decide whether it had been right to baptise them in the first place. Had a mistake been made? Could those genuinely born again then be lost? Such questions stirred up a hornet's nest of doctrinal differences among the missionaries. Before they knew what had hit them, there was trouble on every side and most of the new recruits were disaffected. Some went home, but others transferred to different missions. Satan, with a well-tried ancient plot, attempted to crush the work.

Some new missionaries found the HAM too hard a school; not all were warriors with Studd's standard of singleness. The married ones were barely given time to be together. 'A soldier should only work, and when he is so dog-tired he can no longer continue—then sleep!' said Studd. To add to their difficulties, throughout this whole period funds were always low. This influenced his attitudes, so, like a businessman, he looked for a good return in work and souls saved, from every missionary. Later he regretted this and said, 'We must not organise ourselves on business lines—we're a family.'

Dissension among the missionaries became a running problem. Doctrinal differences, church structure, ordination, baptism, liberty in worship, all were thrown into the arena and tossed about to no one's good. The Home Committee also joined in the general mêlée. The HAM consisted of a collection of people with very strong views—C T leading the way. Few of the recruits were experienced people, and most knew very little of church history or its variety in doctrine.

One young man arrived with the intention of seeing the HAM field preaching the full gospel with the gift of tongues as the sign of the baptism in the Holy Spirit. C T Studd took him to task, saying, 'We don't want any 'denominational truth' here. Preach Jesus Christ only and him crucified.' Another was told to take his 'spiritual toys' elsewhere! Both left.

Entire sanctification became the biggest thorny problem. Studd, a great preacher of holiness, attracted missionaries from Methodist and holiness groups. They were horrified when they arrived in the Congo to find that he had not forbidden the use of alcohol. Drunkenness and native wine were part and parcel of life. Letters flew backwards and forwards to the Home Committee, the temperance faction being very vocal.

For his defence Studd said he wasn't adding anything to the gospel. The Bible only condemned drunkenness and excess and he would not move from that. Later on, as the church grew, it took a different stance and adopted a strong temperance line.

Native dancing became the next bone of contention. Without relenting, the devil raked up controversial issues, one after another. There were fightings within and fightings without, all aimed at diverting the HAM warriors from their principle task. The catalogue of traumas they endured should be warning enough to us today. Satan's strategy hasn't changed.

The war in Europe exercised its own pressure upon the tiny band of beleaguered workers. Their numbers had dwindled, and for eighteen months no new recruits sailed. The few left on the field battled with sickness, as blackwater fever and malaria took its toll. The stranglehold upon the finances seemed set for ever. Discouragement did its own deadly work and strained relationships. As these darts from the enemy tore in among them, Studd said, 'The offensive is always the best defence!' and so with renewed determination he charged at the problems.

Unfortunately Studd lost sight of the real enemy and was more inclined to take his offensive action against people. He seemed so locked into the situation that he could no longer view the actions of others, or his own reactions, in a sober light. His judgements at times seem petty and, worst of all, he continually dragged up old hurts and offences from the past. The simplicity of spirit that he showed in his younger years, especially when in the United States, seemed smothered by old festering wounds and disappointments. Experience had made him less teachable. Outrageous accusations had been levelled at him by those who only desired his harm, and, most painful of all, some of his closest family and friends had turned against him.

Priscilla stood by him, but found his lengthy letters of repeated complaints unwelcome, she refused to publish an article in the HAM magazine to expose the activities of an opponent to their work. Despite her definite views, in November, 1917, Studd wrote to praise her for all she had done.

Studd began to muse on the idea of returning home, but he was never very serious about it. Finally he agreed; the time had come for Alfred, Edith and baby Susan to go. Alfred had shared the brunt of the battle to establish the work. He had proved himself to be a very able, dedicated, hardworking man—an example to all. He deserved the title of co-founder of the mission. His five years in Africa had transformed him from a naïve zealot to a mature missionary statesman. 'Alf is now indispensable here,' Charles wrote to his wife.

When it came to the final farewell, Alfred asked C T to lay hands on him and pray. Whispering in Alfred's ear, he agreed, but only if Alfred did what he said. Placing a chair he asked him to stand upon it and began to pray, laying his hands upon his feet, rather than his head. These two men, so different in character and temperament, were intricately joined in love and admiration.

Alfred went home to find the Home Committee depressed, with faith flagging. The war dragged on and it seemed the little mission was going to be starved to death. The magazine circulation had dropped, but C T retorted, 'If it sinks below 300 we will fight on!' Thank God for his fighting spirit because the devil almost won. Even Priscilla was despondent and could see no hope.

Studd had the most amazing ability to rise up in faith when everything seemed lost. He again encouraged the Home Committee as he had done a few years earlier. At the blackest hour, he sent a cable: 'Many converts — Deti — Wamba 50, Niangara, Nala 100, Forward crusaders fight the devil — shoot traitors not brothers!' He then detailed how, in the face of impossible odds, the victory was being won. Some converts confessed to having eaten men! Precious souls were being rescued from a pit of sin. The miracle-working power of the gospel, producing such fantastic results, proved sufficient reward to sustain them all in the fight.

A new stirring had begun. Studd rejoiced as a welcome freedom came into the meetings in Nala. The worship and praise spontaneously burst forth. The hallelujahs and shouts of victory were almost enough to lift the grass roof of the church! What were C T Studd's critics going to say now? The Christians were dancing in the church! The joy of the Lord so took hold of them, their feet couldn't keep still. Like David of old they danced before the Lord. Well-oiled, shining bodies glinted in the paraffin lamps, as they raised their hands and jumped for joy. How they could sing! Rich powerful voices blended in a natural harmony only heard in Africa.

C T Studd wished to make a tour of the various stations to assess the work. He had said, with little conviction, that he would return home once the task was complete. Niangara, Poko, Bambili and Nala formed a rough square about half the size of England and containing ten tribes. C T had set himself a formidable task for an old man, when many miles would be covered by foot or cycle.

He travelled south out of the Wellé province—which by itself was seven times the size of Belgium—into that of the Ituri. A married couple had opened a station which had become very fruitful. He was full of praise for what he saw in an area that demanded a new language. Since Alfred had left, only six missionaries remained. Despite the restraint upon the work, God encouraged Studd. The Lord had granted him acceptance by the officials, which in turn aided the gospel as the people saw it wise to receive him. They called him Bwana Mukubura—Great White Chief—a title of honour for a greatly respected man. Further land concessions were granted, which could not be utilised then as they were stretched beyond limit, with some trying to cover two or three places at once.

Undaunted, Studd trained and sent out the local Christians in evangelism. He said, 'It's not the shape or size of the blade that counts, it's the sharpness of it.' They turned to prayer and Bible study and saw the clean cut of the word of God do its work. He expected a harvest. He expected labourers. God would fulfil his promises.

CHAPTER TWENTY-SIX

PRISCILLA THE MAINSTAY

THE SPHERE OF CT's final ministry was the Congo, but his vision was the unevangelised world. Priscilla Livingstone Studd actuated the vision. She pioneered the invasion into all the world.

When C T returned to Africa in 1917, Priscilla miraculously received a whole new lease of life. The day following his departure she got up from her bed, cast doctors' opinions aside and never again lived as an invalid. Was this God's response to Charlie's prayers? Or did she suddenly find faith to believe? We do not know.

When the Rev Gilbert Barclay, another of the Studd's sons-in-law, was appointed chairman of the Home Committee, Priscilla found a kindred spirit. He turned out to be a tremendous help to her, putting into action so many of her hopes and plans. Under his guidance the mission took up its vision for the whole world and adopted the new name of Worldwide Evangelization Crusade in 1919.

In 1921, Priscilla, now fifty-seven years old, soldiered on alone, carrying the main burden of the home end of the work. Stormy years had passed since she had seen her husband. Differences, difficulties and heartbreaks had come between,

Priscilla in 1921 — tireless and faithful

but she permitted none of these to divert her from her calling. United with her husband in vision and zeal, she gave her whole life to take the gospel to the unevangelised world.

In 1922 the opportunity came for Priscilla to visit her husband during a holiday abroad. Alfred could see no reason why Priscilla, whose health was stable, should not go and wrote to say so. This evoked a furore. C T, in adamant mood, wrote saying, 'She must not come.' Priscilla proceeded with her plans. He retaliated in a very strongly worded letter,

'Who could take her place at home and what would she do here? Would she learn the language and then go home again? So people say she should be with her husband. Never mind what people say. Priscilla you are needed at home.' He genuinely feared that if she came she wouldn't survive, and knowing that the weight of the mission rested upon her shoulders, it made him insecure.

A visit by Priscilla could have been of great value to the work. She recruited and interviewed candidates; how much better if she had had a personal knowledge of the situation. But another reason loomed larger: Priscilla needed to see her husband. Inside the efficient manager, tender emotions cried out for healing, assuring words. On many occasions she had pleaded with Charlie to return, but he had no mind to do so, although he periodically promised that he would. He complained about her short, infrequent, unloving letters, but failed to respond to the indications of her need.

After a holiday in Cairo, where to the last she hoped he would visit her, she obeyed him and went home. He said, 'We must sacrifice—must give an example.' While Priscilla was in Cairo sick of heart, Charlie, as limp as a rag, lay sick with fever. His planned tour of the Ituri was postponed.

Priscilla dragged herself out of her disappointment and rallied her emotions. The years that followed only widened the gap and saddened them both; love was stifled by sore wounds.

This little episode sowed seeds of contention between Studd and Alfred Buxton. Alfred, no longer the inexperienced boy, voiced his own opinions and very lovingly confronted Studd, who rarely took such without fighting. In Studd's mind differences of opinion were akin to lack of loyalty.

With the progressive realisation of Studd's vision, the need for more property became apparent. At different times the buildings, either side of number 17, were up for sale. Should they step out and buy? The battle of faith waged to and fro. Ignoring the chronic state of their finances they went ahead and bought. Now, besides the Studds' home, they owned offices and accommodation for missionary candidates, each property possessed by faith.

In 1923 the vision for other unevangelised fields became a reality. The WEC opened a second mission field among the tribes of the Amazon. The first three men went like David going up against Goliath, ill-equipped and certainly no match for the enemy. Despite the fiercest opposition, God helped them and provided for all their needs.

In every work of faith, actions are taken which to the casual onlooker are foolish. No one studying the bank statements for the WEC in 1923 would have thought it wise to diversify the work into other fields. But that is not the way of God. Every advance of his kingdom is by faith, against impossible odds, and looks like rash naïvety. The act of going is the step of faith that puts into motion the spiritual forces which generate all that is needed to do God's will. The step of obedience, whether buying a house or going to the Amazon, can helpfully be visualised as switching on the power to a huge water wheel. The acts of faith are like the power that keep it turning to generate and guarantee a constant supply. Faith comes before provision.

Actions of faith open the door to God's storehouse which has ample supplies for a continuing work of faith. God does not supply for plans that might be, but all heaven is engaged when faith plugs into the heavenly supply.

When the three men went to the Amazon, the expansion into a new field did not restrict the growing needs of the Congo. When God allows us to have access to his purse, we discover that it has elastic sides and faith is the power that stretches them.

Later, two more exceptionally difficult regions were entered: the fanatical Muslim areas of Central Asia and Arabia, where workers attempted, at first unsuccessfully, to live and travel with the Bedouin tribes.

Implicit childlike faith in God, rooted in the infallibility of his word, controlled and directed all of Priscilla's decisions. Hers was no second-hand faith. From the beginning she had cast her all on God. When she sailed to China as a young woman, with a full, exciting life ahead of her, she said, 'I was given a passport but firmly told, "This is no guarantee of your security. You may have to lay down your life." ' Priscilla then had the responsibility to make sure her family understood; if she were killed they were to make no fuss. It was on that condition she sailed. The strong shoot of faith planted so many years earlier now bore large, mature branches. Her faith reached in all directions.

Priscilla continued in faith and in obedience, even where she didn't understand. Faithfully she laboured and trusted God to cause all things to work together for good. She could have been a disappointed, lonely, sour old lady, but she chose the opposite and was one-hundred-per-cent loyal to her husband. She spoke well of him and with all her energies worked with him to see his vision accomplished. Where he unwittingly caused difficulties, through old age, distance and awkwardness of character, she smoothed things over and poured oil on troubled waters. Ignoring the impossibilities, she proclaimed the favour and promises of God with unwavering faith in the face of stupendous tasks.

Lily Searle, an ardent young missionary recruit, remembers Priscilla's love. Although Priscilla had a forthright way of speaking and a very upright bearing which could appear forbidding, her motherly, compassionate manner won all who knew her. Lily said, 'She showered the candidates with love and "unnecessary" goodness. She did all she could to make life pleasant. Mrs C T suggested we went to beautiful places to gather special memories to reflect upon when we reached the Congo.'

Priscilla took a very special interest in the candidates. She personally interviewed each one, and her letters to the 'would-be hopefuls' were full of encouragement. Like a person with a good eye for business, she never allowed an opportunity to slip by. Evelyn Crow, a student at the Redcliffe Bible College, was engaged to be married to a young man who had decided to volunteer for the Congo. Priscilla urged Evelyn to also volunteer. By the following post applications forms were in her hand!

Prayer was a way of life for Priscilla. The late night, or early morning, found her in prayer. Once when reading, '*Pray ye* therefore the Lord of the harvest, that *he will* send forth labourers into his harvest' (Mt 9:38), her attention was drawn to the words, 'Pray ye' and 'he will'. She said, 'Is that all, Lord?' 'Yes, can you believe that?' 'I do.' She had heard from God; the issue was settled. She would pray and he would do it.

Throughout the mission, prayer alone was established as the means by which recruits were found and funds received. The prayer meetings crackled with life when Priscilla, playing the harmonium, led out with victory songs. For the students, the times of intercession were the highlight of the week. With a kindly geniality, Priscilla led the meeting. Adjusting her lorgnette, she would open her Bible and speak with fervour. Exhorting the people to trust the Lord, she claimed God's promises and declared his victory. These faithful prayer warriors were spiritual co-workers with the missionaries in their fight against the powers of darkness.

Priscilla, a woman of great personality and endowed with many gifts, snatched time between her activities to be mother to her daughters, and later, grandmother. Somehow this motherly side of Priscilla didn't quite meet the needs in her own daughters. Edith, a more retiring personality, never felt she knew her mother well. There was little time to stop and just be a family.

Susan, Priscilla's granddaughter, remembers staying at

number 17. From the high windows she watched a firework display at the Crystal Palace and enjoyed granny's bountiful table. Priscilla's Irish largesse overflowed into good entertaining. So often an army of guests sat round her table. 17 Highland Road was open house to the servants of God from every corner of the world.

Edith and Pauline both had their first child in the Congo. Priscilla must have shared a kindred spirit with them as she remembered her own experiences in China. Like any mother she sent all the good advice she could. Edith said, 'Mother equipped me for every contingency, even with advice for dealing with a cleft palate.' With the family divided between the Congo and England, Priscilla never had the privilege of holding Pauline's first child. How her heart must have broken when she received the news of his death. Only in prayer could she find solace when she longed to take Pauline in her arms and comfort her.

Family weddings were always marred by the absence of father, or, in the case of Edith, mother. The lack of togetherness in their family life could have been a source of resentment for Priscilla. But remarkably she found grace to overcome and said, 'We are in a war; separation is part of the cost. God's war needs warriors.' And we know the price she paid; it cut deeply into her heart and emotions. Priscilla walked in the benefits of a brave decision; she would not allow any hurts or injustices to cloud her fellowship with God.

The continuous triumph in her life was only possible because she decided to give place to continuous death. Daily, life presented her with endless opportunities to be self-pitying and bitter. But how did she react? She devoted herself to the Saviour; with a positive dynamic she served him and the mission cause.

A worldwide mission required worldwide support. The American council had been founded by the visits of Alfred Buxton, Priscilla, and the deputation secretary, Miss C

Brandon. After initial difficulties the American council became most effective in sending missionaries worldwide.

Priscilla wished to see as many councils established as possible, but she first concentrated upon Australia, New Zealand, Canada and South Africa. Miss Brandon went to New Zealand and Australia, and Priscilla followed her. Away from home for months at a time she travelled from city to city, challenging the church with the need of the world. She covered over 31,000 miles in Australia and another 6,000 in New Zealand. Altogether she took 272 meetings. At the end she could rejoice—thirty applied to the mission.

All her journeys were ventures of faith. Priscilla didn't take a salary from the funds or claim travelling expenses. Every leg of the journey was accomplished by faith. No offerings were taken at any meetings, but she carefully recorded all sums received which were forwarded in total to headquarters. She said, 'Some of you may think that gold was showered upon me—no—it wasn't.' All money, even a few pence for a stamp or a train fare, was paid into the Melbourne council to send candidates to England.

She would preach, usually twice a day, then sleep at different homes almost each night of the week. The days passed in study, writing letters, preparation and prayer. To all who meet her, she was a lady—so kind and thoughtful. They would never forget the WEC or its most valuable representative.

After Australasia there was South Africa. When challenged to go, Priscilla had no money for the venture. Then the Lord reminded her of a small sum she had in the bank. She said, 'I did not feel that I could pray for God to send money miraculously with that there,' so she went ahead, financing the tour from her own funds. Priscilla, as energetic as any young woman, travelled 3,000 miles, visiting eight centres and conducting 59 meetings. To make it all worthwhile, she found twenty-nine willing applicants.

Priscilla and workers at the Keswick Convention

With all her energy she pushed forward the mission on every front. CT's letters to her bewailed the lack of personnel. Tirelessly she went out after recruits, using all her ability to locate, select, train, and send the best she could find.

Without ever making appeals for money, Priscilla did more than anyone to raise finances. By the grace of God she had a flair for producing money. Stringent financial conditions continued throughout her lifetime, but this led her deeper into faith. She talked faith, prayed faith and received the fruits of faith.

In their early years Charlie had joked about her attempts at organising him, but now Priscilla came into her own as a first-class organiser. She took the business side of the mission in hand. How she waded through all the correspondence that passed through the office is a mystery, especially in addition to the volumes dealt with in her own home. She familiarised herself with the minutest details, both of correspondence and finance. Her intimate knowledge of all associated with the mission, whether as subscribers, helpers, intercessors, or candidates, was truly wonderful.

The tenth anniversary of the mission in 1923 showed Priscilla at her amazing best: a first-class, powerful preacher. She had everyone on the edge of their seats at the Central Hall in London. Priscilla lifted her voice and preached on 'Songs of Deliverance', beginning with the Song of Deborah: '. . . they shall rehearse the righteous acts of the Lord . . .' (Judg 5:11). Then she told the 'wonderful story of a wonderful mission'. She continued with the Song of Moses: '. . . he hath triumphed gloriously . . .' (Ex 15:1). Then came the Song of David: 'For by thee I have run through a troop: by my God have I leaped over a wall' (2 Sam 22:30). Priscilla could have continued all afternoon telling of the wonders God had done for them in answer to faith. She illustrated her talk with true stories of how they got their money, buildings, men and new mission fields. She had run through a troop, she had leapt over a wall;

nothing could stand in their way. 'Everything is possible for him who believes' (Mk 9:23).

Priscilla urged her audience with all her might:

> Strain every nerve and muscle in every direction! Let's put ten times more effort into the work, and in return you shall receive ten times more mental, spiritual and physical exhilaration. For by my God we shall have ten times more faith.
>
> God wants you to make a flying leap! Are you ready? Up, this is the day!

She closed, 'I have ordained you to go and bring forth much fruit. The world needs men with a world vision. I pray you get that world vision today.'

Charles made his attitude to his wife's ministry well known. He said, 'I would rather have my wife stand on a platform with me than any other man I know. I can always depend upon her to bring a dynamic message from God. I've never heard a woman, and very few men, talk like her.'

Priscilla barely had time in the middle of her whirlwind of a life to consider herself. Like her husband, she had put her own desires at the end of her list of priorities. Her life was spent for God's glory; she poured it out joyfully. No doubt the sadness of differences with her husband tinged her happiness, but it never blunted her usefulness. She served her husband and the mission in her abandoned service of God.

In 1928, Priscilla, a most determined lady, now aged sixty-four years, decided to visit her husband. She wanted to see him once more before they both went to glory, and she hoped to persuade him to return home. Charles, far from happy about the idea, feared for her life—perhaps unnecessarily—but accustomed himself to the thought of the visit. With Norman Grubb, who had married their daughter Pauline, Priscilla and a small party arrived in Ibambi by car.

What a strange meeting, after so many years. A husband and wife who lived in two different worlds but with the same goal, now looked at each other. Their two different worlds had made them two different people. Priscilla, a world-travelled, accomplished missionary speaker, met a totally indigenised servant of God. He belonged to the Congo.

Priscilla was unprepared for the vast change she found in Charlie. She said, 'He seemed to be the ghost of my former husband—yet behind his frailty I found a giant mentally and spiritually.' She stayed there just thirteen days. Special meetings were organised, and in her own excellent style she preached to the Africans, so many of whom she knew intimately in prayer. God wonderfully blessed those meetings. Priscilla was the amazing attraction. They came from far and wide to see Bwana's wife.

She attempted to bring C T home, but he refused every entreaty. He would die in the Congo. She protested; she did not want to return home alone. But Studd insisted. The parting was terribly hard—what could anyone say? They walked silently to the waiting car. She got in, with her face set and her eyes fixed in front. As the car turned around, she did not look back.

The following year, on the 5th of January, 1929, this courageous lady went to be with the Lord. While on holiday in Spain with a close friend, she was suddenly taken ill and after only one day's sickness went into glory. The WEC lost its main architect and builder.

It is amazing what God can do through those who are fully yielded to him. Priscilla knew she could do nothing without the grace of God, but how sobering to see what God did accomplish. Without Priscilla there would be no WEC. St Augustine said, 'Without God we cannot. Without us, God will not.'

CHAPTER TWENTY-SEVEN

INCOMING FRIENDLY

DURING THE VIETNAM war the US troops never knew when or from where the next attack would come. At the sound of artillery the lookout yelled over the loudspeaker, 'Incoming!' Everybody dived for cover. Sometimes the shout would be, 'Outgoing!' and the company relaxed as their own guns fired on the enemy.

An ex-Vietnam soldier tells of the time when the speaker bellowed, 'Incoming friendly!' What is 'Incoming friendly'? In the confusion of war, unwittingly, the gunners shelled their own troops. But the horror of the story is, incoming friendlies can kill.[3]

In the early days the young mission existed in a state of prolonged famine: of funds, personnel, and confidence— conditions guaranteed to expose every weakness. Those who were strong became stronger; those who were weak soon capitulated, finding no resources within themselves. As the winds of adversity and the battering of 'incoming friendlies' hit the Heart of Africa Mission, dozens and dozens of good-hearted missionaries fell by the wayside. Controversies, shortages, sickness and disillusionment carried them away, while a determined handful dug their heels in deeper and fought on. What follows is the confusing story of incoming friendlies.

Back in 1921 when Alfred had returned to Nala, Studd moved on to Ibambi to find amazing spiritual hunger. Hundreds sought the Lord, and at nearby Imbai 1,500 sat in the sun for two hours to hear the gospel and then came back for more. They built their own church to seat 1,250. Studd had found his El Dorado. He made Ibambi the new head-quarters and remained there till his dying day.

Alfred again attempted to encourage C T to return home, but it fell upon deaf ears, along with the entreaties from the Home Committee. 'What, go home? Never! God told me to come and he hasn't said go.' Studd began to feel his authority was being questioned and became very wary of Alfred. Alfred went the second mile to allay his fears, even resigning as co-founder, but to regain Studd's confidence was almost impossible.

Isolated, and feeling the lack of approval from the Home Committee and that of his own wife, Studd became doubly defensive. Alfred tried so hard to help him but only got caught in the crossfire. Accusingly he wrote, 'It looks as if Alfred is the loving one—I am the ogre.' Although agonising with these problems, Charles, for a considerable time, could see no other substitute leader than Alfred.

While Alfred and Edith had been in England, Pauline, with her new husband, Norman Grubb, joined her father in the Congo. After C T Studd's death, Norman led the home end of the mission and then wrote *C T Studd, Cricketer and Pioneer*. They had a somewhat cool reception from Studd. Pauline found her father's behaviour incomprehensible, especially when he preferred another missionary to nurse him during a bout of illness while he sent her and Norman to a far station. Norman too had his difficulties with C T and early on discovered it impossible to differ with him and remain friends.

The trauma of strained relationships caused Charles Studd eventually to turn to Norman. Matters came to a head. C T needed someone to represent him to the committee. He wrote letters, organised and persuaded till Norman finally capitulated. Sadly the young couple buried their first child, Noel—CT's grandchild—on his first birthday, before they left the Congo.

Certain landmarks stand out clearly during the final years of Studd's life. To understand them properly, each one must be seen against the back-cloth of the life of an impassioned zealot. Studd never flinched from urging himself and others on in the fight against the powers of darkness. He only lived to see souls saved and the forward march of the gospel in unevangelised fields. This 'raison d'être' consumed him, captivated his workers and carried them along. In this one thing they were united.

When a party of American missionaries arrived in the Congo in 1924, their presence stirred up a hornet's nest of doctrinal differences. They were Calvinists, and the rest of the workers on the field took a directly opposite stance. Studd never did accept the Calvinist tenet, 'Once saved always saved.' He insisted that holiness of life and a hatred of sin were fruits of repentance to be continually evidenced before new birth could be assumed. No recipe could be found to make this oil and water work together. Within weeks the Americans had left to work elsewhere.

If that had been the end of the matter the situation could have passed without comment, but the Home Committee were appalled that the first party of American recruits had been disaffected. Priscilla and Alfred had visited the USA and put a great deal of time and effort into establishing the US office. The committee tended to blame Studd for mishandling the affair and turning away promising workers and supporters.

The problem rumbled on and gave the Home Committee a solid reason for mistrusting Studd's judgements. He was an extremist; possibly a man of a more conciliatory nature could have found a harmonious answer.

Priscilla, as the secretary of the committee, had the painful task of conveying their thoughts to her husband. Looking at the difficulties from their perspective they concluded that C T was too old and sick; he needed a rest. Infuriated at such suggestions, his reply, written to Priscilla in such hot words, only furthered the distance in their marriage. He refused to return home to those whom he considered no longer respected or loved him. Priscilla, utterly discouraged and barely able to continue with the responsibility, wanted to quit.

The strain of these affairs bore heavily upon Studd. Weary, unwell and far too old, he battled on. After preaching and singing for hours—he had a lovely tenor voice—he stood to say the benediction and fell back into his chair. In a concerned letter he wrote, 'I had a sort of seizure.' He believed he had little time to live. He suffered with periodic pain and swelling in his hands and feet. A year previously a doctor had diagnosed a heart problem, besides an enlarged liver and partially congested lungs. Ignoring his aging body he refused to give in. Before him lay an unfinished task.

The next hurdle the fragile mission had to overcome concerned the strange business of the DCD.

Studd, a bit of an eccentric, had always been obsessed by militarism. He quoted Rudyard Kipling and the warring speeches from Shakespeare. To him the great soldiers of history were figures to admire and emulate in the Spirit. Most of the booklets he wrote are on warring themes, with covers depicting soldiers with swords drawn, defeating the foe. Studd lived to trample the devil underfoot and bring in the glory of the Lord. With his pen he sent thorns into the sides of Christians living at ease. 'Come along, enlist at once as one of Christ's frontiersmen to struggle and fight and pray, to cast down the works of darkness and win the well-fought day. Surely better one thousand times to die at the front, than to live at the rear,' he wrote.

His final words in his famous booklet *The Chocolate Soldier* were sent like mortar shells to blast the sleepy church.

> Come, let us restore the "Lost Chord" of Christianity—heroism . . . Christ himself asks . . . "Will you be a malingerer or a militant? To your knees, man! And to your Bible! Decide at once! Don't hedge! Time flies! Cease your insults to God, quit consulting flesh and blood. Stop your lame lying and cowardly excuses. Enlist!" Live for Christ, be a militant, a man of God, a gambler for Christ and a hero.

He formed an 'order' of those missionaries and converts who signed a vow or 'cut an oath', saying, 'Henceforth I DCD (Don't Care a Damn) for anything, save the glory of Jesus, obedience to God and the evangelisation of the world.' So he launched the DCD and tenaciously defended it in the face of outraged disapproval. He took impish delight in shocking strait-laced people. Most missionaries signed, and there followed a wave of dedication among the local believers as they cut the oath unto death—

    not to commit adultery
    not to lie
    not to deceive

A fear came upon them lest they break their oath. Sinners returned from their backsliding, and long-standing Christians put their lives in order. Shining faces, singing and joyful hearts evidenced changed lives.

A spirit of prayer swept through their gatherings, and at Ibambi C T's own life of total sacrifice drew the missionaries to new depths of commitment. Every evening he held a meeting in his house at 8.00pm. The meetings were supposed to finish at 10.00pm, but they would go on and on. The group learned what it meant to be living sacrifices. He expounded Romans 12:1–2 and Hebrews 11 on the heroes of faith. He explained from 1 John 3 and 2 Corinthians 5:17

how absolutely impossible it was for believers to continue in sin. He had no time for theological terms; it was experience that counted. Isaiah 35:8 was his standard: 'And a highway will be there; it will be called the way of Holiness. The unclean will not journey on it; it will be for those who walk in that Way; wicked fools will not go about on it' (Is 35:8, NIV).

The challenge of the DCD exploded in the committee. Studd demanded that each person should sign the DCD oath as only DCD's could truly represent the crusade. The stronger the opposition, the more unyielding he became. Norman Grubb went to the Congo as an ambassador of peace, but because he was essentially one with Studd in what he stood for, though not in the way he expressed it, he ended up signing.

Studd wrote a booklet, *The DCD*, written in provocative terms and decorated with gruesome skull and crossbones—a most unlikely presentation for a thoroughly worthy sentiment. The Home Committee could be excused for refusing to publish it. Undeterred, Studd pressed on and published it privately.

What could have been an extremist episode turned into a calamity. Scandalised, many British Christians rejected Studd and the WEC. The committee tried to rescue what remained of the mission on the home end. Studd failed to appreciate the devastation his 'incoming friendly' caused. The committee, conscious of their widening responsibilities and need for a broad-based acceptance, did their best to nullify the problems the DCD created.

*   *   *

May Willson arrived in Ibambi in 1920 to become CT's secretary. Living and working in close proximity with the grand old man gave her ample opportunity to appreciate his strengths and weaknesses. He suffered far more attacks of fever than most, probably because he didn't use a mosquito net. With his breathing frequently difficult, he preferred to cover himself with an insect repellent and sleep on the verandah, 'where he hoped for the best.'

May says, 'Studd, in his weakness, continued to be an inspiration to us all. He threw himself into the work. Whatever the Lord asked him to do, he did.' His light was the last out at night and the first on in the morning. He poured himself out for the Lord. His example put all to shame. Though old and sick he continued to pray early each morning with the Africans, and he even travelled through the night in a carrying chair to preach in far villages. He covered large distances at hours when no African would normally venture out. So as not to waste time on the journey, he had his Bible and note book at hand.

The final controversial issue which brought open division was C T Studd's dependence upon morphine. His attitude to the drug must be seen in the context of the times in which he lived. Most medicine chests then contained tincture of laudanum, an opium derivative, and morphine and quinine were frequently included in a traveller's medical kit. From his earliest days Studd had done his own doctoring. He made no secret of his taking morphine—he even injected himself in front of the missionaries. The Africans called it Bwana's quinine. When challenged, he said, 'It's the only thing I've found so far to master my pain and weakness, to give me strength to speak the gospel.' His one intention was to muster every last ounce of energy to do the task in front of him. He dreaded becoming a liability to the workers—they had enough to do—so he took morphine with the same attitude as a diabetic takes insulin.

He wrote,

God works in wonderful ways. I was bad with fever and in bed with a temperature of 102.6°. Crowds came, so I gave myself an injection of mophine. I went out, took the meeting which lasted five hours or more, came back smiling with no temperature at all . . . People are getting right with God, at considerable sacrifice.

In unsophisticated medical situations morphine would be most useful. It is a very effective pain-killer and could have helped C T to continue with his crippling workload. Medical opinion is that it may not necessarily have had a deleterious effect upon Studd. Morphine dependency in medical conditions is not automatically a sinister thing. For Studd morphine would have brought him immediate relief from his malarial headaches and heart pains. He may have assumed it was the answer to all pain, including the severe pain associated with gall-stones. Grubb suggests he suffered with this condition.

A violent storm of controversy broke out. Studd declared, 'I've never taken morphine for "pleasure".' That statement is entirely in keeping with his life of total sacrifice. He insisted to his daughter and son-in-law that only with its help was he able to keep going. Undeterred, he contined with his open requests for the drug and refused to hear the condemnation of those, far away in their comfort, who knew nothing of his need. Obviously some missionaries were disturbed and out of genuine love for him desired his retirement. They wished to see the old man go home, where, with proper medical treatment, he could recover his health.

Studd wrote to Pauline and Norman, 'I've not increased the dose—I only take sufficient to keep me active.' It is possible that his dependency was well-controlled, although the patient is never the best judge of the situation.

We know his lifestyle did not indicate addiction as we understand it today. He did not neglect himself or cease from work. To his last days he was particular about his clothing, however old it may have been, and his shoes were always polished. Those close to him said he was a perfect gentleman;

it shone out from him. And work? If anything he was a 'workaholic', tireless in his service of God. C T's soldier-spirit and devotedness to Christ set such a standard that Jim Grainger, a new missionary, wondered how he would fare. The local Christians said, 'he works all the time!' Even when he went to the toilet he took his books and was known to compose hymn verses while in that particular seclusion! If he woke in the night he was ready for work with his books all around him. He reached for the lamp, and a handy board, which he pulled across his knees, served as a desk.

During these years he completed the translation of the New Testament into Kingwana. In 1926 he said, 'I've nearly completed Galatians. Praise God! Romans-Revelation finished.'

His output of letters was prodigious. He wrote to all the missionaries on their various stations. They were letters as from a loving father to his children. Jim Grainger said,

He addressed his letter, 'My dear Sonny,' and ended it, 'Your loving old father C T S.' In between were words of praise to the Saviour and encouragement to spur one on to deeper love and dedication to the Lord. His life was a splendid example of sacrifice, shaming us by its reality and the shallowness of ours. He wrote, 'I'm not as efficient as the youngsters but I am more efficient than an absentee! God knows all about my health, need of rest and many things regarded as absolutely necessary to enable one to live in these regions. I gladly laugh at being without them and rejoice in a living death with a marvellous joy in order to fill the place that others have left unoccupied.'

Charles Studd pushed himself beyond the normal limits of human endurance. He knew no other way; to his dying day he lived a total death to himself. What he preached, he was—a living sacrifice.

*　　　*　　　*

Alfred came to Ibambi to be reconciled with Studd. Their broken relationship did WEC much harm and cast further doubts upon Studd's leadership. How could these two who had loved so deeply, separate?

For a few days the two men hedged in superficial niceties and then had it out. Studd did not want Alfred on the Home Committee; he feared he would compromise on principles Studd held dear. He refused his olive branch. From his perspective, Alfred should have come asking for forgiveness. But he had genuinely forgotten the issues that grieved Studd.

Herbert Jenkinson, a missionary whom Studd repeatedly commended for his faithfulness and loyalty, watched these proceedings and was unwittingly drawn in. Saddened by what he had seen, he returned to his house a troubled man. He felt someone from C T's own family should come and take responsibity for him, especially as he knew C T Studd took morphine. On one occasion he had watched him inject himself.

He wrote to Norman Grubb. Swamped with the problems, Norman was unable to respond. Back home the mission funds dwindled till every cable sent said, 'No funds received.' The DCD, the doctrinal controversy, and now the public knowledge of Studd's drug dependence, shrivelled up the last remaining support. Of the family, only Norman and Pauline remained with the mission.

The grave situation brought Norman to write to his father-in-law explaining that the DCD expression and the news about him taking morphine was involving them in endless explanations and justifications. He proposed that C T should take up a suggestion he himself had earlier made, and resign along with Norman and Pauline, thus freeing the mission to continue without the embarrassments. He also proposed that DCD should be made to stand for, 'I don't care if I die for Christ.'

Eventually a deputation was sent to see him; two returning

missionaries, Buckley and Evening, went with Roome and Thynne, both committee members. They planned to attempt to bring him home, but if they did not succeed it was agreed they should establish another mission. In actual fact the two groups never met.

Buckley and Evening travelled south and located in Stanleyville province at the courtesy of the Baptist Mission, and so began the Unevangelized Fields Mission.

The whole committee resigned and supported them. Schism rent the WEC in two. Later they were joined by the missionaries in Brazil and a group from the Congo.

Norman Grubb acted admirably. Loyalty counts high in the courts of heaven. Already Norman had told C T his judgement, but he could not allow the situation to go unchallenged. With his brother-in-law, Colonel Munro, he went into the office at 17 Highland Road as C T Studd's representative and removed the files. The WEC would go on.

The tattered remains of the WEC fell into Norman Grubb's lap. The incredible story of its resurrection is told in *After C T Studd*. Today the WEC owes its existence to his incredible faith and hard work.

In Ibambi the fierce reality of the situation hit hard. Herbert Jenkinson, Studd's representative in the Congo, with his wife, who had lovingly cared for Studd for years, were among those who resigned and joined the UFM. (C T's nurse Edith Paton, went with them.) There are no winners in these divisions—each one who went, and those remaining, received ravaging wounds.

Only six months later Studd entered into glory. Busy to the last moment—he hardly had time to die—after a few short days of sickness, with 'Hallelujah' on his lips, the old warrior met his Lord.

Storm clouds filled the skies and torrential rain fell upon the pall-bearers as they carried his body to the graveside. Draped with the DCD flag he had designed, the coffin was lowered into an African grave. Almost 2,000 national Christians lifted their voices in songs of praise. Studd had wanted no solemn funeral. It was a fitting end for the old warrior. His life's work complete, he could rest in peace.

Tributes poured in from all over the world to honour God's fighter, but none were more precious than that from Alfred Buxton;

C T's life stands as some rugged Gibraltar—a sign to all succeeding generations that it is worthwhile to lose all this world can offer and stake everything on the world to come. His life will be an eternal rebuke to easy-going Christianity. He has demonstrated what it means to follow Christ without counting the cost or without looking back.

C T was essentially a cavalry leader and in that capacity he led several splendid charges ... and forwarded evangelisation to an extent that we cannot properly gauge.... He personified the heroic spirit, the apostolic abandon, which is easy to lose from the work of Christ.

The cavalry leader cannot have all the gifts of an administrator, or he would not have the qualities necessary to lead the charge. In this simple fact is the explanation of the shortcomings some might point out. If there were these, they were in reality the exaggeration of C T's unique qualities; his courage in any emergency, his determination never to sound the retreat, his conviction that he was in God's will, his faith that God would see him through, his contempt of the arm of flesh and his willingness to risk all for Christ. But these are only as Froude wrote of Carlisle, 'the mists that hang about the mountain'. Men who want no mists must be content with the plains but give me the mountain. It will be but a little while, and the mists will evaporate, the mountain will stand out in all its grandeur. I myself owe an enormous debt to him. From him I learned that God's ideal of a saint is not a man primarily concerned with his own sanctification; God's saint is fifty per cent a soldier. So we and thousands more will continue to thank God for the soldier-life he lived and the soldier-death he died.

A great man had passed into his reward. He had lived the kind of life that attracted attention. Revealed in its gaze were his clay feet as well as his heart of gold. But that day, as heaven received him into his final reward, the spotlight fell upon his heart of gold as he glorified his master with much fruit.

CHAPTER TWENTY-EIGHT

MUCH FRUIT

BOTH CHARLES AND PRISCILLA STUDD have left their mark upon the history of modern mission. Both possessed pioneer determination as tough as granite. Neither one would give in. Whatever the devil threw against them, or whatever 'incoming friendlies' blasted at their feet, they were not to be moved.

Studd was first and foremost an evangelist. He never concentrated on building the church—that waited for another man's gift. He devoted himself to extensive evangelism. There is no point in saying what he should or shouldn't have done—he did what his gift enabled him to do.

His warrior character led him into many a skirmish. Like King David, he was a man of war. When David wished to build a house for the Lord, God only allowed him to prepare the materials and left the building task to Solomon, his son. Charles Studd prepared much 'material' for building the house of God. Thousands of black Africans enjoy heaven today because Studd and those with him obeyed the Lord. When he entered into his reward, God allowed another to build his church. Just as the Lord looked upon David's heart, so he looked at Charles Studd. He saw his heart of total devotion and absolute obedience; that was so much more important to God than the aberrations in his character. The Lord honoured him for his heart.

God writes history in the terms of human personality. The book of Genesis gathers around eight men. The Bible presents epochs and eras; but at the centre of each is a personality, and generally the man is the key to the age.[4] Studd certainly wrote history, with every ounce of his energy and drop of his sweat. Today the heart of Africa worships Jesus—debauchery and black magic have all but gone.

C T Studd never neatly fitted into anyone's classification. He was destined to be a founder. The singleness of his heart put him in a category of his own. He rushed in where others feared to tread, and said, 'I come to do thy will O God.' His body was available; the will of God would be done.

The difficulties of world evangelism are legion. But difficulties give way to determined men. The price is high. God does not want partnership with us, but ownership of us.[5] Studd knew he was bought with the blood of Jesus. His Owner had absolute use of his property.

Charles Studd gave his fortune away and in his own lifetime received a hundredfold back into the mission finances. Throughout his life he did not personally lack funds. He regularly received gifts of £500 or £1,000 for him to use as he saw fit. For the most part it went to support his work and provide for the other missionaries. His own personal needs were minimal. He lived with locally-made furniture and fittings to the end of his days.

Studd's life was given up to death even while he lived. He was living out a principle: life must flow out of death. It seems that his wish to die in the heart of Africa grew into a deliberate plan. Studd saw his life as a seed which when sown into African soil would produce a hundredfold. With his own eyes he witnessed God's faithfulness. The hundredfold return began to flow in as other young men and women came joyfully to dedicate their lives for the salvation of the lost, making the way for new fields to open.

Since C T and Priscilla went to their reward, WEC has sent missionaries to more than forty countries of the world. The total number of active workers today exceeds 1,100. But that is not the whole story, because out of WEC grew the Christian Literature Crusade with over 600 workers following the principles of faith and complete devotion to Jesus which were exemplified by the Studds. In addition must be added the numbers of the Unevangelized Fields Mission, which arose out of the schism. They did a great work in the Congo before the Simba uprising of the early 1960s, and they now work in five other countries.

Today WEC is still sending out men and women to the remaining unevangelised peoples of the world. Their programme is one of expansion until those from every tribe and nation shall stand around the throne of God to glorify the Lamb.

It is good for us to realise that Priscilla and Charles Studd were people with ordinary problems and with the same capacity to act and feel as ourselves. They were not superstars from an unattainable realm. Their massive achievements should not intimidate us. When we view them as they truly were—ordinary flesh and blood with the power of God working through them—there is no reason why God shouldn't do the same again. All he needs is an abandoned life.

Do not count yourself out through lack of gifts. God can equip you with any ability to do his will. Remember, in his early days C T was no great orator. His gifts developed with use. Although he had a very able mind, he did not excel at administration. Priscilla did. The impulsive side of his character always remained. It made him somewhat erratic but in God's hands more able to throw caution to the wind and dare for God.

His one great asset was his passionate all-consuming love for Christ. Jesus came first in everything. His pre-eminence far exceeded any love of self, comfort, worldly possessions or intimate relationships.

In God's hand C T Studd was the arrow of the Lord, whittled down to the bare necessities—no fuss, frills or fancies, and with only one desire: to go.

C T Studd in 1929

IMPORTANT DATES IN THE LIVES OF C T STUDD AND PRISCILLA

Charles Thomas Studd born	2nd December, 1860
Converted	1876
Priscilla Livingstone Stewart born	28th August, 1864
CT Trinity College, Cambridge	1880
Cricket career	1880–1884
CT received his call to China	November 1884
Sailed to China with Cambridge Seven	February 1885
Priscilla converted in Ireland	1885
Gave away his fortune (aged 26)	13th January, 1887
Married Priscilla Livingstone Stewart	1888
Returned from China	1894
Ministry in US and UK	1895–1900
Sailed to India	1900
Home at Hyde Park Gardens	1906
CT received his call to Africa	1908
CT went to Sudan on exploratory visit	1910
CT and Buxton sailed for Africa	3rd January, 1913
First Heart of Africa Mission base established	1913

First baptismal service in Niangara	1915
CT returned home for more recruits	1916
CT returned with party including Edith	1917
Edith and Alfred married	1917
Remarkable fruitfulness in the Ituri	1919
Title Worldwide Evangelization Crusade adopted	1919
Norman Grubb and Pauline went to Congo	1919
Mrs Studd went to USA	1920
Alfred Buxton returned to Congo	1921
American Council begun	1921
Ibambi opened	1921
Tenth anniversary forty missionaries on the field	1923
Expansion into other fields began	1923
Priscilla went to Australia and New Zealand	1924
Priscilla went to South Africa	1925
Priscilla visited Ibambi	1928
Priscilla died in Spain	15th January, 1929
CT died at Ibambi	16th July, 1931

SOURCES OF INFORMATION

BIBLIOGRAPHY (ARRANGED IN
CHRONOLOGICAL ORDER)

(An * indicates that the book was believed to be in print in January 1988)

The Christian's Secret of a Happy Life. Hannah Whitall Smith. (Fleming H Revell Company, 1870).

China's Spiritual Need and Claims. Hudson Taylor. (Morgan & Scott, 6th Edition 1884).

A Story Retold. 'The Cambridge Seven'. Arthur T Polhill-Turner. (Morgan & Scott/China Inland Mission, 1901).

From the Cape to Cairo. Ewart S Grogan and Arthur H Sharp. (Hurst & Blackett Ltd, 1902).

1910 Report of Commission 1: Carrying the Gospel to all the non-Christian World. John R Mott. World Christian Student Federation, New York.

Quaint Rhymes for the Battlefield, by a Quondam Cricketer (C T Studd). (James Clarke & Co, 1914).

Hudson Taylor and the China Inland Mission. Dr and Mrs Howard Taylor. (China Inland Mission, December 1918).

The First Seven Years of the Heart of Africa Mission. Alfred B Buxton. (Heart of Africa Mission, 1920).

The First Ten Years of the Heart of Africa Mission. Alfred B Buxton. (Heart of Africa Mission, 1923).

Why God used D L Moody. R A Torrey. (Banner Publications, 1923).

Out for the Uttermost. (WEC, 1928).

Priscilla Livingstone Studd (Mrs C T Studd). (WEC, 1929).

Reminiscences of Mrs C T Studd, by her husband. (WEC, 1929).

Charles T Studd, Cricketer and Missionary. Thomas B Walters. (Epworth Press, 1930).

*C T Studd, Cricketer and Pioneer. Norman Grubb. (Lutterworth Press, 1933).

Floods on Dry Ground. Eva Stuart Watt. (Marshall, Morgan & Scott, 1939).

After C T Studd. Norman Grubb. (Lutterworth Press, 1939).

Alfred Buxton of Abyssinia and Congo. Norman Grubb. (Lutterworth Press, 1942).

Christ in Congo Forests. Norman Grubb. (Lutterworth Press, 1945).

Successor to C T Studd. Norman Grubb. (Lutterworth Press, 1949).

A Mighty Work of the Spirit. Norman Grubb. (WEC, 1950).

Mighty through God. Norman Grubb. (Lutterworth Press, 1951).

This is That. Norman Grubb. (Christian Literature Crusade, 1954).

*The Cambridge Seven. J C Pollock. (Inter-Varsity Fellowship, 1955).

*Why Revival Tarries. Leonard Ravenhill. (Bethany Fellowship Inc, 1959).

This is No Accident. L Moules. (WEC, 1965).

Congo Saga. David W Truby. (Unevangelised Fields Mission, 1965).

Going Through with God. Lily Searle. (WEC, 1965).

*Millionaire for God. John T Erskine. (Lutterworth, Faith and Fame series, 1965).

Reluctant Missionary. Edith Buxton. (Lutterworth Press, 1968).

Once Caught, No Escape. Norman Grubb. (Lutterworth Press, 1969).

Mama Harri—and no nonsense. Mary Harrison. (Oliphants, 1969).

With God in Congo Forests. David M Davies. (WEC, 1971).

*C T Studd, Cricketer and Missionary (illustrated). E C Julian. (WEC, 1973, 1988).

*Fool and Fanatic? Jean Walker. (WEC, 1980).

*C T Studd, Cricketer and Crusader. Kathleen White. (Marshall Pickering, Heroes of the Cross series, 1985).

BOOKLETS AND PAMPHLETS

The Heart of Africa. C T Studd (For Africa Inland Mission).

The Jehad of Jesus. C T Studd (HAM/WEC).

The Laugh of Faith. C T Studd. (HAM/WEC).

*The Chocolate Soldier. C T Studd. (HAM/WEC, CLC USA).

For the Shame of Christ, and the lands over the sea. C T Studd. (HAM/WEC).

*Christ's Etceteras. C T Studd. (HAM/WEC, Facsimile edition 1988).

Constitution and Policy of Heart of Africa. C T Studd. (HAM).

Dawn in the Devil's Den, 1913–1915. C T Studd. (HAM).

Progress in the Heart of Africa, 1914–15. A B Buxton. (HAM).

To the Soldiers of God. Gone or Going to the Heart of Africa. C T Studd. (HAM).

World-wide War, Real or Sham? C T Studd. (HAM).

The Gates of Hell Prevailing. Why? And how to close them. C T Studd (HAM).

'Our Bit!' Let's do it quickly! C T Studd. (HAM).

Life Story of an Eton, Cambridge and All-England Cricketer. C T Studd. (HAM/WEC).

A Journey of Miracles, 1916–1917. C T Studd. (HAM).

A report of the inception and growth of the Heart of Africa Mission, 1913–1917. (HAM).

Gardeners', 1918. A B Buxton. (HAM).

Nala Missionary Methods. A B Buxton. (WEC).

Little Darkies' Budget. Alfred Buxton. (WEC).

A Missionary Romance. The Heart of Africa Mission. Mrs C T Studd. (WEC).

The Three Flies. Edith Buxton. (WEC).

Chocolate and Cream. Edith Buxton. (WEC).

The Attack — Fourteen Days with Mr C T Studd in the Heart of Africa. Rev W F Roadhouse. (WEC).

Parent's Price, by one who has paid it. (WEC).

Baragwani, A Congo Saint. (WEC).

The DCD. C T Studd. (Printed privately, 1928)

A Statement of Facts. For private circulation only. (WEC, 1931).

Life out of Death. Account of the resurrection of the Heart of Africa Mission from its moment of greatest weakness in 1931. (WEC).

Union Church, Ootacamund. Survey of a Century. 1855 – 1955. J K Keary. (Wesley Press).

Reluctant No Longer. Edith Buxton. (Printed privately, 1973).

Politics, Economics and the Problems of Protestant Church Leadership in Africa. William McAllister. (Thesis, University of Aberdeen, 1986).

MAGAZINES

*WEC magazine 'Worldwide' (formerly 'The Heart of Africa', 'World Conquest'). (WEC bimonthly, 1913 onwards).

ARCHIVES

Personal correspondence owned by the trustees of WEC International.
Of the Overseas Missionary Fellowship.
Of Hudson Taylor and valuable assistance from A J Broomhall.
Of the Africa Inland Mission.

PERSONAL INTERVIEWS WITH:

Mr and Mrs Charles and Lily Searle
Miss Marjorie Cheverton
Mrs May Willson
Mrs Ida Grainger
Dr Timothy Robson
Mr Herbert Jenkinson
Lady Susan Wood, C T Studd's granddaughter

AND IN ZAIRE WITH THOSE WHO HAD KNOWN
C T STUDD:

Pastor Autani
Mama Utalo—Ibambi
Baba Singi—C T's houseboy
Mama Gbalanga
Pastor Kadobo
Pastor Manbenecobo
Pastor Danga
Pastor Undugu—did duplicating for C T Studd
Baba Mbenze
Baba Lutiru—at Nala
Pastor Mapuno—at Imbai, a man with a shining face

NOTES

Introduction

1. Quoted by David Shibley in 'Church Growth Magazine', September 1987.

Chapter 6

2. For the non-British reader 'public' schools refers to the elite of private schools.

Chapter 27

3. *Edification*, volume 10, no 4. Edification Ministries, USA.

Chapter 28

4. *Why God Used DL Moody*. R A Torrey. (Banner Publications, 1923).
5. *Why Revival Tarries*. Leonard Ravenhill.

INDEX

Abraham   162
Adamson, Mr   73
Africa Inland Mission   153, 155–156, 159–160, 166, 167, 169, 174, 185, 194, 246
After C T Studd   233
Alexandria   63
Alimasie   183
Amazon   214
Ampthill, Lord & Lady   120
Ananias and Sapphira   78
Anglo-Indian Evangelisation Society   118
Arabia   215
Arebi   182
Asia (Central)   215
Augustine, St   222
Australia   30, 46, 218
Azandis   147, 148, 166

Bahr-el-Ghazel   146, 147
Baleka   168
Bambili   194, 209
Bangala (language)   177, 188, 197, 201
Baptist Missionary Society   191, 233
Barclay (nee Studd), Dorothy (daughter)   122, 126, 175
Barclay, Rev Gilbert   211
Barnardo, Dr   77
Batstone, Mr   155, 160, 185, 186
Bazande   192

Beauchamp, Lady   61
Beauchamp, Montague   53, 65, 73
Bedouin   215
Belfast   83
Belgian Congo   146, 148, 155, 156, 165–169, 177, 178, 195, 197, 200, 206, 214, 216, 217, 222
Bible Society   73
Bihar   16
Booth, William   44, 77, 78, 84, 85
Booth-Tucker, Commissioner   78, 90
Bourne, Mr (British Consul)   76
Bowers, A J   197
Bradshaw, William   131, 144, 147, 148
Brandon, Miss C   218
Brindisi   63
Bristol   77
Buckley, G F   233
Burroughs, Miss J   87, 88, 95, 97
Buxton, Alfred   150, 153, 155, 160, 163–76, 169–179, 184–186, 189, 195–197, 199–204, 208, 212, 213, 218, 224, 225, 232, 234
Buxton, Barclay   139, 150, 153, 155, 164, 165
Buxton (nee Studd), Edith (daughter)   122, 128, 130, 136, 150, 153, 164, 196, 200, 202, 204, 208, 216,   217, 224

249

Cairo 213

Calais 61

Calcutta 118

Calvinism 225

Cambridge 29–32, 35–36, 37, 48, 49, 50, 53, 53, 150, 151

Cambridge Seven, The 57, 61, 64, 65, 92, 110

Canada 218

Carmichael, Amy 123

Cassells, W W 38, 65, 73

Cheam, Surrey 16

China 38, 48, 50, 51, 53, 58, 59, 61–108, 110, 113, 115, 117, 135, 145, 215, 217

China Inland Mission 48, 50, 53, 55, 64, 67, 77, 81, 100, 103, 105, 108

Chocolate Soldier, The 141, 227

Christ's Etceteras 176

Christian's Secret of a Happy Life 41

Chungking 73, 75

Church Army 37

Church Missionary Society 131, 145–149, 152, 164

Clark, Mr 185, 186

Colombo 63

Columbia 110

Congo (river) 159, 191, 199, 202

Coonoor 120

Crow, Evelyn 216

Curzon, Lord 120

Darwinism 48

David (king) 209, 214, 220, 236

DCD, The 226–228, 233

Deborah (judge) 220

Deti 208

Dover 157

Drugs 104, 229–231, 232

Drury Lane (theatre) 20, 21

Dublin 19, 77

Dungu 172, 179, 180, 182, 183, 184, 185–187

East Sudan Evangelical Mission Committee 152

Edinburgh 57, 58, 71, 129

Edwards, Sir Herbert 162

Elk Hill Lodge 118

Eton (school) 16, 23, 24–25, 27, 32

Evening, D V 233

Faradje 184, 185

Gee, Billy 167

Germany 196

Gibraltar 234

Gideon (judge) 148, 153, 165, 175

Goliath 214

Gordon, General 174

Grace, Dr W G 30

Grainger, Jim 231

Grand National 16

Grenfell, Sir William 35

Gribble, Mr 167

Grogan, Ewart 167

Grubb, Noel (grandson) 217, 225

Grubb, Norman 165, 221, 224, 225, 228, 230, 232, 233

Grubb (nee Studd), Pauline (daughter) 122, 202, 217, 221, 224, 230, 232

Grunne, Count de 188, 192, 198

Gwynne, Bishop 146, 147

Han (river) 65

Han-chung 65, 66, 73

Hankow 65

Havergal, Frances Ridley 42

Heart of Africa magazine 201, 208

Heart of Africa Mission 159, 175, 176, 194, 198, 200, 206, 207, 223

Highland Road, Upper Norwood 154, 199, 214, 217, 233

Hogg, Mr 70

Hoh-chau 87, 95

Holland, Mr 77

Hong Kong 63

Hoste, D E 38, 53, 62, 65, 71

Hsi, Pastor 88, 95–96, 104

Hudson Taylor, James 48, 52, 53, 55, 56, 57, 58, 63, 66–67, 69, 72, 73, 75, 79, 90, 91, 92, 93, 100, 107–108, 246

Hungtung 95

Hyde Park Gardens 17, 21, 33, 37, 109, 110, 113, 124, 128, 134–136

INDEX

Ibambi   221, 224, 227, 233
India   16, 76, 77, 117–124
Indiana   110
Ituri (forest)   180, 184
Ituri (province)   209, 213

Japan   80, 81, 108
Japan Evangelistic Band   139
Jenkinson, Herbert   232, 233, 246
Jericho   165

Kentucky   110
Khartoum   131, 135, 142–146, 148,
   149, 174
Kilo   166, 169–180, 182, 185
Kingwana (language)   231
Kipling, Rudyard   226
Knox College   111
Kumm, Dr Karl   126, 127, 128,
   129–130, 131, 144, 151

Lake Albert   164, 165, 168
Lake Victoria   164
Leicester   54
Lisburn   83
Liverpool   58, 126, 133, 134, 142
Livingstone, David   47
London   17, 20, 21, 23, 24, 32, 34, 37,
   39, 50, 52, 55, 56, 61, 77, 109, 135,
   144, 166, 220
Lucheng   105
Lungan   83, 90, 96, 97–108

Madras, Bishop of   120
Madras (port)   118
Madras (state)   120
Mahagi   166, 167, 169
Manchester   103
Mangbetu   192
Masindi   164
McCarthy, Mr   50
Medje   192
Melbourne   218
Meyer, Rev F B   54, 60
Miller, Mr   185
Moffatt, Mr   185
Mombassa   159
Mongolia   91, 92

Moody Bible Institute   77
Moody, D L   18, 19–22, 23, 24, 30, 34,
   35, 36, 49, 76
Morris, Mr   155, 160, 185
Moses   220
Mott, John   110, 129
Moule, Handley   54
Muller, George   77, 195
Munro, Colonel   233

Nairobi   160, 163, 164, 166
Nala   193, 194, 200, 202, 205, 208,
   209, 224
Nebraska   110
Nepoko   192
New Zealand   218
Niam Niams   148
Niangara   186–192, 194, 204, 208, 209
Nicholson, John   162

Ohio   110
Ootacamund   118, 119–122
Oxford   50, 53

Parker, Mr   65
Paton, Edith   233
Paton, John   47
Paul (apostle)   66
Penang   63
Pennsylvania   110
Peter (apostle)   66, 96
Ping-Yang   68, 71
Poko   194, 209
Polhill, Arthur   57, 64, 65, 67, 71, 72
Polhill, Cecil   57, 59, 64, 65, 67, 71, 72,
   91, 92
Polygamy   204
Price-Hughes, Hugh   60
Prince Albert   44
Punch   29
Pygmies   192

Queen Victoria   15, 43–44, 58

Radcliffe, Reginald   55, 58
Radstock, Lord   192
Rampley, Mr   155, 160
Red Sea   63

Redcliffe Bible College 216
Roome, W J W 233
Ruscoe, Alfred 135
Ryle, Bishop 48

Salvation Army 41, 44, 48, 77, 78, 81, 84, 86, 90–91, 94, 100, 137
Samson (judge) 69
Sankey, Ira D 18, 19, 49
Schweinfurth, Dr 187
Searle, Lily 215, 246
Semme 182
Shakespeare, William 226
Shanghai 63–64, 80–83, 90, 94, 95, 108, 113
Shansi (province) 73, 83, 91
Shaw, Archdeacon 146
Sherbourne School 124
Shunteh 107
Simba uprising 238
Singapore 63
Smith, Rev Frederick 64
Smith, Hannah Whitall 41
Smith, Stanley P 31, 37–38, 40, 50, 51–54, 55–59, 65, 71, 90, 95, 100, 101, 102, 103–105, 177
Solomon (king) 236
South Africa 218
Spain 222
Spurgeon, Charles 48
Staines, Mr T 118
Stanleyville 159, 233
Studd, Dora (mother) 15, 16, 23, 25, 27, 51, 52, 56, 57, 94, 96, 107, 109, 124, 128, 138, 154, 175
Studd, Edward (father) 16–18, 20–23, 26, 27, 34, 68, 75, 83
Studd, George (brother) 24, 31, 32–35, 80, 91, 117
Studd, Herbert (brother) 22–23
Studd, Kynaston (brother) 24, 27, 30, 31, 32, 35, 37, 50, 51, 52, 57, 61, 110
Studd, Priscilla 72, 78, 81–89, 91–92, 93–109, 112–124, 128, 133–143, 153–162, 173, 175, 187, 191–192, 194–195, 197, 202, 207–208, 211–222, 225–226, 236, 238
Studd, Paul (son) 102–103

Student Volunteer Movement 110
Sudan 130, 131, 138, 144, 146, 148, 150, 152, 155
Sudan Evangelistic Mission 147
Suez 63, 158, 159
Sutton (nee Studd)—later Munro—Grace (daughter) 101–102, 122, 126, 192
Sutton, Martin 174, 192
Switzerland 124

Tedworth, Wilts 16, 17, 22, 23, 24–27
Thynne, Rev A V 233
Tibet 92
Tientsin 96
Tirhoot 76, 117

Uganda 164
Unevangelized Fields Mission 233
Union Church, Ootacamund 118–119, 121, 124
United States 46, 110–116, 118, 207, 225

Vietnam 223
Vincent, Mr 19–21, 117

Wamba 208
War Cry 78
Welle (province) 185, 209
Welle (river) 189
Wetherby, Mr 26, 27
Willson, May 228–229, 246
Wolsely, Lord 177
Wood (nee Buxton), Lady Susan (grand-daughter) 208, 217, 246
World Christian Student Federation 129
World Missionary Conference 129, 144
Worldwide Evangelization Crusade 212, 214, 218, 222, 228, 232, 233, 238

Yangtze 65
Yorkshire 144

If you would like further information on the ministry of WEC today please contact:

UK: WEC International, Bulstrode, Gerrards Cross, Bucks, SL9 8SZ

OR:

Australia WEC International, 48 Woodside Avenue, Strathfield, NSW 2135

Canada WEC International, 37 Aberdeen Avenue, Hamilton, Ontario, L8P 2N6

New Zealand WEC International, PO Box 27264, Mt Roskill, Auckland 4

Republic of South Africa WEC International, PO Box 47777, Greyville, 4023

USA WEC International, Box 1707, Fort Washington, PA 19034